MELEAGER: The Poems

MELEAGER: *The Poems*

Jerry Clack

BOLCHAZY-CARDUCCI PUBLISHERS

Cover design: "Fritillaria Meleagris"

FOREWORD

I hope through this unpretentious volume to render Meleager's poetry accessible to undergraduate audiences. Although generally admitted to be an important Hellenistic literary figure, both as a poet and as the compiler of an anthology which transmitted many Hellenistic epigrammatists to modern times, Meleager has suffered eclipse.

The reasons for the dimming of his reputation are several and understandable. First, there is a widespread feeling that epigrammatic poetry is too ephemeral to command serious attention. Next, although there have occasionally been separate editions of Meleager's poetry, Meleager is in the popular mind buried in the labyrinth of the sixteen books of the *Greek Anthology* and so retrievable only with difficulty. And finally—up to the present generation, at least—the paederastic nature of some of the epigrams has effectively banished Meleager from the undergraduate curriculum.

In deference to our poet it should be made clear that Meleager is from a paedogogical point of view a good introduction to Greek poetry at the undergraduate level. The total of his 132 epigrams are encompassed in little more than 800 lines, allowing for a complete reading of his oeuvre within a very short time. The grammar is simple. The epigrams, with the exception of the introductory poem, are short. And the vocabulary, although imaginative, is limited and easy to master. The verse is elegiac couplet, introducing the student to dactylic verse, the most prevalent metrical form in Greek poetry.

The text I have followed here is that established by A. S. F. Gow and D. L. Page in their splendid study *Hellenistic Epigrams* (Cambridge 1965); I have included occasional emendations which Gow and Page rejected on textual or other grounds but which satisfy the sense of the poetry.

My view of Meleager has been influenced especially by Henri Ouvré's *Méléagre de Gadara* (Paris 1894), whose sensibilities and assessments of Meleager's poetry are still invaluable, and by Carl Randinger's *Meleagros von Gadara* (Innsbruck 1895), noteworthy for its study of Meleager's style and "art of variation".

Rather than append a separate bibliography, I have cited important articles concerning the interpretation of many of Meleager's epigrams at appropriate places in the commentary.

The order in which the epigrams are presented is that of Gow and Page. It has become the accepted sequence, grouping the epigrams by subject matter. Although it might at first seem tempting to seek some sort of chronological, biographical, or even alphabetical arrangement (each has been suggested at one time or another), such an undertaking would be highly subjective and open to immediate criticism in the absence of internal evidence justifying such tampering.

In keeping with the Gow and Page edition, the following epigrams have been omitted from the Meleagrian canon: *A. P.* 5. 2, 99, 189; 7. 13; 9. 363, 453; 11. 223; 12. 79.

Finally, it should noted that although this edition refers throughout to "Gow and Page", it was D. L. Page who undertook the lion's share of the commentary on Meleager.

I wish to express my thanks to Anthony O. Leach II, Ronald Polansky, Karen Hoover, and Catherine Weisinger for their inestimable assistance in preparing this volume.

Εὐκράτεω Μελέαγρον ἔχω, ξένε, τὸν σὺν Ἔρωτι
καὶ Μούσαις κεράσανθ᾽ ἡδυλόγους Χάριτας.

(*A. P.* 7. 416)

TABLE OF CONTENTS

INTRODUCTION

The Life of Meleager

Knowledge of Meleager's life is preserved for us in four epi-
grams: *A. P.* 7. 417, 418, 419 (Selections 2, 3, 4) and the anony-
mous *A. P.* 7. 416 (printed in this edition on page vi). Scholars
generally agree that the first three were written by Meleager him-
self. Although the information these epigrams convey is meager
and repetitious, it still exceeds in quantity the evidence tradition-
ally provided by such autobiographical exercises. We know sub-
stantially more about Meleager than about many other Greek
literary figures.

Meleager tells us that he was a Syrian, that the name of his
father was Eucrates, and that he was born at Gadara. Although
politically insignificant, Gadara had a prominent role in anti-
quity's literary tradition: it was the home of Menippus, the third-
century Cynic philosopher and author of a sarcastic prose and
verse medley which became known as Menippean satire, and of
Philodemus, a first-century Epicurean philosopher represented by
thirty-four epigrams in the *Greek Anthology*. Meleager states, how-
ever, that it was the city of Tyre which reared (ἤνδρωσεν) him, and
that in later years he was awarded citizenship at Cos, that is, on the
island if not in the very city which had welcomed a number of his
Hellenistic literary predecessors, such as Philetas and Apollonius.

Meleager's dates can be established only in the most general
terms. The scholiast tells us that the poet flourished ἐπὶ Σελεύκου
τοῦ ἐσχάτου, during the reign of the last Seleucid king, presum-
ably Seleucus VI Epiphanes Nicator. Since this Seleucus held the
throne only from 96-95 B.C., Meleager is given a scant *floruit*.
There is little internal evidence in Meleager's *Garland* to guide us.
An epigram by Antipater of Sidon (*A. P.* 7. 493) refers to the
Roman sack of Corinth in 146 B.C., the latest identifiable histori-
cal date. On the other hand, Philodemus, Meleager's countryman
who published in or about 80 B.C., is not represented in the col-
lection. Since the reign of Seleucus Epiphanes Nicator is the only
firm date available to us, we can assume only that Meleager may
have lived at least into the early years of the first century.

Commentators who have scrutinized the autobiographical epi-

1

grams ask why Meleager would write as many as three, and, if he did, whether he wrote them at different periods of his life. Satisfactory answers have not been forthcoming, nor is such questioning demonstrably productive.

It is troubling that none of the autobiographical epigrams mentions the *Garland* (*Stephanos*), the literary work on which Meleager's fame rests and thanks to which his poetry has been preserved for posterity. The epigrams refer only to his Menippean *Graces* (Χάριτες) and apparently to amatory poems (Ἔρωτα ... χάρισιν [*A. P.* 7. 419. 3-4] and μέτρον ἐρωτογράφον [*A. P.* 7. 421. 10]). These latter efforts, we must assume, are at least in part the epigrams to be found in the *Greek Anthology*, that is, the *Palatine* and *Planudean Anthologies*.

As for the *Graces*, we have only two inconclusive statements in that invaluable repository of exotic information, Athenaeus' *Doctors at Dinner* (Δειπνοσοφισταί):

> In his work entitled the Graces Meleager of Gadara said that Homer—insofar as he was a Syrian by birth—portrays the Achaeans as abstainers from fish in spite of the fact that there was a plenitude of them in that region of the Hellespont. (4. 157B)

> Meleager, the Cynic, in his Symposium writes as follows: "in such a situation he assigned him a heavy task of drinking toasts, twelve deep pots" (that is, chytridia). (11. 502c)

Little can be extracted from these paragraphs except for the existence of a work by Meleager entitled *Symposium*, which may have constituted a portion of the *Graces*. Athenaeus' reference to Meleager as a κυνικός must have been based on a reading of the *Graces*, since Meleager's epigrams include only two statements concerning his philosophical allegiance: "we all have one fatherland" and "Chaos begot all men" (*A. P.* 7. 417. 5-6), both commonplaces.

The Garland of Meleager

Scholars have given as much attention to the structure of

Meleager's *Garland* as to his poetry. While critics long ago dismissed the notion that the *Garland* was the first collection of diverse epigrams in the ancient world, their terminology maintains Meleager's suggestion that such collections are "garlands" of poetic conceit, so that the term "anthology" continues to be used to describe them. Meleager, as best we can determine, was the first to identify the poets he included in his *Garland* with flowers and plants. It is an apt conceit, since Meleager displays a fondness for flower-metaphors and flowers in his own poetry.

Scraps of papyrus testifying to earlier anthologies are not sufficient to indicate from which of them, if any, Meleager drew, or what exactly were his sources for the forty-seven poets he included in his collection. Only on one point does there seem to be consensus as to these papyri. R. Reitzenstein ("Inedita Poetarum Graecorum Fragmenta," *Index Lectionum Rostochiensis* [1891/2] II and *Epigramm und Scholion* [Giessen 1873]), observing that a book rather inelegantly entitled the *Heap* (Σωρός) is mentioned in the scholia to *Iliad* 11. 101, postulated that prior to the *Garland* the epigrammatic poets Asclepiades, Posidippus (mentioned in the scholium), and Hedylus (all third century writers) had "published" their verses in a common volume. This was the *Heap*, not a product of indiscriminate dumping but of careful winnowing and sorting. Reitzenstein's conclusion is based on the fact that these three poets often appear in clusters in the *Garland* and are mentioned together in Meleager's introduction to the *Garland*: "both Posidippus and Hedylus, wild flowers of the meadow, and the anemones of Sicelides" (a nickname for Asclepiades) (*A. P.* 4. 1. 45-46). Most important was Reitzenstein's observation that some of the epigrams in the *Garland* bear double ascriptions attesting Meleager's uncertainty as to which of the three poets might have been the author. Meleager did not depend only on the Σωρός, but did use it as one of his sources.

There is, too, a third century papyrus (Milne, *British Museum*, §60) containing the poetry of Posidippus, and of others whose names, tentatively restored, are not found in the *Garland*. This anthology was apparently intended as a wedding gift—perhaps for Arsinoë I, wife of Ptolemy I Philadelphus. The poems are characterized as "leaves and flowers from a garden fountain." Such terminology suggests sympotic poetry in which the revelers were garlanded, while the "garden fountain" no doubt refers to a cultured and polished "Muse," studied and refined poetry. The papyrus anthology is entitled *Mixed Epigrams* (Σύμμεικτα Ἐπιγράμματα), denoting the variety of epigrams it contained.

Suggested publication dates for the *Garland* range from the first decade of the first century B.C. back in time to the last decade of the second century, since the *Garland* apparently was known at Rome to Q. Lutatius Catulus (*cos.* 102) (Cicero, *de Or.* 3. 194).

Organization of the *Garland* is equally conjectural, but at least allows for several reasonable suppositions based on evidence in the *Greek Anthology* itself. The task is complicated by the fact that the *Anthology* in its present form has passed through the hands of a number of later editors who have shaped and reorganized it, as one might expect, to suit their own tastes. Still, there remain in the *Anthology* identifiable groups of epigrams which can be termed "Meleagrian sequences," allowing us to speak of a poem as being in a "Meleagrian context" and thus to posit an organizational system for the *Garland* (see A. Cameron, "The *Garlands* of Meleager and Philip," *GRBS* 9 [1968] 323-49). These "Meleagrian" poems in the *Greek Anthology* amount to about 4,000 lines (approximately 800 epigrams) without counting the additional lines necessary for ascriptions to individual poems and for titles. Although the length of Greek texts included in a single papyrus roll is still hotly disputed, a total of 5,000 lines would by anyone's admission be too many to be accommodated in a standard Greek "book." We can reasonably expect, as a result, some sort of subdivision. The reference to Meleager's work, in the plural, as *Stephanoi* by the later anthologist Philip of Thessalonica also argues for multiple books in the *Garland*.

It is thus not improbable that Meleager's *Garland* consisted of four books which contained (excluding 45 poems found in the *Planudean Anthology*) 270 ἐροτικά, 290 ἐπιτύμβια (sepulchral epigrams), 135 ἀναθηματικά (dedicatory epigrams), and 50 ἐπιδεικτικά (declamatory epigrams). These thematic divisions represent four of the seven divisions to be found in the *Anthology* of the sixth century anthologist Agathias—the only four divisions to which the poets of Meleager's *Garland* contributed. Books of such a length could have reasonably fit on a standard papyrus roll. Within this structure Meleager appears to alternate major poets (Asclepiades,

Callimachus, Leonidas, and himself) with lesser lights so as to emphasize thematic and verbal links. These poets and others represented in the *Garland* are discussed at length in my annotations to Meleager's account of his anthology (*A. P.* 4. 1) . The *Garland* is dedicated to Diocles in Selection 1 (*A. P.* 4. 1. 3) and again in the κορωνίς (Selection 129, *A. P.* 12. 257. 5).

A few words remain to be said about the transmission of the *Garland* to modern times, since there is clear evidence that collections of Greek and Latin epigrams were produced throughout antiquity. Those of significance for Meleager are:

(1) The *Stephanos* of Philip of Thessalonica, published about 40 A.D. during the reign of Caligula, and composed of epigrams written after Meleager completed his own *Garland.* Philip's anthology contains the work of Philodemus and so assists us in the dating of Meleager's *Garland.* His *Stephanos* shows evidence of literary schools, such as that of Leonidas of Tarentum. The introduction to Philip's *Garland* is extant (*A. P.* 4. 2), so that its contents can be reconstructed with some confidence.

(2) In the middle of the sixth century, apparently during a revival of interest in epigrammatic poetry, Agathias Scholasticus published an anthology which the *Suda* refers to as a *Cyclus.* Its introduction has been transmitted to us as the third and penultimate epigram in Book 4 of the *Greek Anthology.* The main thrust of Agathias' preface is not, as in the case of Meleager and Philip, a listing of poets represented in his collection, but a lengthy encomium of the Emperor Justinian.

(3) The fates of Meleager's, Philip's, and Agathias' anthologies converged at the beginning of the tenth century (900 A.D.) when Constantine Cephalas, the foremost ecclesiastical representative at the Byzantine court, produced an anthology that drew on all three and added, as one might anticipate, individuals from other anthologies which were in vogue at the time.

(4) Next, at Constantinople in 1299 A.D. the monk Planudes completed a collection of epigrams which was collated into seven books and is referred to as the *Planudean Anthology* (*Anthologia Planudea*). The *Anthology*—that is, Planudes' own copy—has survived as *Cod. Ven. Marcianus* 481. It appears to have been the only anthology which remained in circulation in the fourteenth, fifteenth, and sixteenth centuries.

(5) At the end of the sixteenth century a far more encompassing collection was discovered in Heidelberg (*Codex Palatinus* 23), containing substantial portions of Cephalas' anthology: the introductory poems to the anthologies of *Meleager, Philip,* and *Agathias* (Book 4), as well as epigrams of the following classes: amatory (Book 5), dedicatory (Book 6), sepulchral (Book 7), declamatory (Book 9), hortatory (Book 10), satirical and convivial (Book 11) and the *Musa puerilis* (Book 12). The manuscript itself had been transcribed around 980 A. D. by four scribes. It is accompanied by *scholia* (marginal annotations) and exegeses. The text is also lemmatized (glossed) by a critic of considerable learning.

The *Palatine Anthology*, as it came to be known, gained considerable renown. The manuscript was presented as a gift to Pope Gregory XV in 1623 by Maximilian of Bavaria, and thus found its way into the Vatican library where, to its misfortune, Vatican librarians bound it in two volumes. In 1797 Napoleon, triumphant from his Italian campaign, demanded the manuscript as a prize of war. Two decades later, concurrent with the signing of the Treaty of Paris in 1815, return of the manuscript was sought and obtained, but only the first volume (containing all but the last two books) found its way back to Heidelberg, while the second and smaller volume remained in the Bibliothèque Nationale in Paris. Not until 1911 did K. Preisendanz offer the world an excellent photo-reproduction of all fifteen books (*Anthologia Palatina codex Palatinus et codex Parisinus phototypice editi*), thus reuniting a much travelled manuscript. Complete texts of the *Palatine Anthology* had been available, however, at an earlier date: the editions of F. Jacobs (*Anthologia graeca sive poetarum graecorum lusus ex recensione Brunckii* [Leipzig 1794-1814]), of J. F. Dübner-E. Cougny (*Anthologia Palatina* [Paris 1864-90]), and H. Stadtmüller (*Anthologia Graeca* [Leipzig 1894-1906]) are a sine qua non for scholars.

It is customary in modern times to append a sixteenth book to the *Palatine Anthology* containing 388 epigrams included in the *Planudean Anthology* but not found in the larger work.

The Epigrams

The greatest injustice that can be done to Meleager is to present his poetry out of context, removed, as in this volume, from the environment of his *Garland*. One of the most attractive features of Meleager's poetry and, as a matter of fact, of much of Alexandrian poetry is its enthusiasm for literary precedent. Meleager's determination in the *Garland* to meld tradition with innovation is clearly demonstrated where he arranges sequences of epigrams to show how several different poets can, while expressing much the same sentiment, manipulate motifs and themes so as to vary, flavor, and give a characteristically novel turn to each poem. Meleager is careful to place one or more of his own epigrams at the end of such sequences, demonstrating that he unhesitatingly set his own talents on a par with the best.

In a volume devoted to Meleager, it would be cumbersome to supply in every instance the epigrams on which Meleager's own are based. Still, there are instances in the annotated portions of this edition where these sequences are noted—occasionally with the text included—to illustrate Meleager's inventiveness and originality. From the substantial literature on the Hellenistic practice of variation, this volume makes extensive use of Walter Ludwig's "Die Kunst der Variation im hellenistischen Liebesepigramm" (*L' Épigramme grecque*, Fondation Hardt, Entretiens XIV [Vandoeuvres-Génève 1967]) and of Sonya Lida Tarán's *The Art of Variation in Hellenistic Epigram* (Leiden 1979). Tarán's investigation embraces dedicatory, epideictic and funerary epigrams.

Wherever one may place Meleager in the hierarchy of Greek poets, one must concede that he is the best of the poets represented in the *Greek Anthology*, and that in terms of ability to achieve "Hellenistic variation," although he stands at the end of several centuries of practice and experimentation, he is the most versatile. A majority of Meleager's epigrams are of an erotic nature, but precisely what makes them attractive to readers is his ability to assimilate a variety of motifs from earlier poets and to make these themes and motifs support and illustrate his particular brand of *Liebesepigramm*.

Many of his epigrams are written in the first person, so that frequently the poet and the "lover" become synonymous. This technique is so successful that at times the artificiality of the situation is forgotten, and the apparent conviction of the poet- lover predominates. We should remember, however, that we are not reading personal confessional poetry, but verses intended for recitation amongst a circle of friends or perhaps patrons of the poet. Meleager displayed his work in a "garland" to insure that the variational aspects, not the sentimental ones, would be foremost in his readers' thought.

As Daniel H. Garrison (*Mild Frenzy* [Wiesbaden 1978]) points out, it was Meleager's creative imagination which enabled him to impart to his epigrams the emotionalism and sentimentalism that distinguished him from his predecessors. Meleager was a good enough poet to create "belief" in a genre which tended to avoid deeper emotions, so that he worked against the expectations of the genre. In numerous epigrams, as Garrison points out, Meleager represents love as an inner experience, while his Hellenistic predecessors spoke of it as an external force. Even Meleager himself at times represents love as a fleet, if not always plump, youngster:

ἐστὶ δ' ὁ παῖς γλυκύδακρυς, ἀείλαλος, ὠκύς, ἀθαμβής,

σιμὰ γελῶν, πτερόεις νῶτα, φαρετροφόρος.

(Selection 37: *A. P.* 5. 177. 3-4)

This is the traditional aspect, as are descriptions of love's symptoms:

ὀστέα σοι καὶ μοῦνον ἔτι τρίχες.

(Callimachus, *A. P.* 12. 71. 3)

or of the comast's frenzy:

κἀγὼ πὰρ προθύροις νίσσομαι ὑόμενος

τρωθεὶς τῆς δολίης κείνης πόθῳ·

(Asclepiades, *A. P.* 5. 189. 2-3)

or when it is materialized as praise of a woman or a pubescent boy.

As Garrison explains, however, while earlier Hellenistic epigrams contain little erotic language which implicates the whole person, Meleager often uses phrases or words which suggest deeper involvement. So it is that Meleager may be said to be "within the Hellenistic tradition, but not wholly of it." Meleager expands the meaning of such common words as ψυχή (it had never before been fully involved in sentimental love), of κραδία, of σπλάγχνα. The soul (ψυχή) comes to represent the inner man; it is envisioned as the seat of love, a love which engages the poet completely: "Half my soul, Andragathus" (Selection 81: *A. P.* 12. 52. 2) or "in you is all the vitality left to my soul" (Selection 108: *A. P.* 12. 159. 2). In a number of epigrams Meleager would have us believe that love affects our vital interior, thus recreating on a romantic level the Platonic suggestion that love is "an essential function of the soul."

Love not only is internalized, but it engages the mind as well. Rather than a diversion, as it is often represented in Hellenistic epigrammatists, it is an activity which nourishes the imagination, awakens memory, and induces dreams. It is serious business:

καί μ' ἔτι νῦν θάλπει μνήμης πόθος, ὄμμασι δ' ὕπνον
ἀγρευτὴν πτηνοῦ φάσματος αἰὲν ἔχω.
(Selection 117: *A. P.* 12. 125. 5-6)

Such engagement carries Meleager one final step, in which the beloved is not only described in the terms of divinity and compared to a god or goddess, but is invoked with a prayer:

χαῖρε Πόθων ἀκτῖνα φέρων θνατοῖσι, Μυΐσκε,
καὶ λάμποις ἐπὶ γᾷ πυρσὸς ἐμοὶ φίλιος.
(Selection 105: *A. P.* 12. 110. 3-4)

In short, as Garrison demonstrates, involvement with the beloved becomes complete:

Ἢν ἐσίδω Θήρωνα, τὰ πάνθ' ὁρῶ· ἢν δὲ τὰ πάντα
βλέψω, τόνδε δὲ μή, τἄμπαλιν οὐδὲν ὁρῶ.
(Selection 95: *A. P.* 12. 60. 1-2)

This is a marvelously concise epigram which compares favorably with Catullus' *odi et amo.*

One problem with interpreting Meleager's poetry is that his more than one hundred and thirty epigrams are not uniform in their treatment of subject matter, in outlook, or in level of creativity. Such unevenness must be attributed in part to the demands of epigrammatic tradition, which occasionally overpower Meleager's natural creativity. For example, the proliferation of lovers in Selection 78 (*A. P.* 12. 256) was a common trope among the earlier epigrammatists, whose traditional procedure was to use multiple names. But Meleager writes groups of epigrams to one person as well, such as those to Heliodora, Zenophila, and Myiscus. These distinguish him from other epigrammatists and are for modern audiences his more successful undertakings.

The sexual elements of ancient literature which scholars have scrutinized in recent years are relevant as well to Meleager's poetry. It is instructive to observe Meleager's treatment of his love objects, for instance, in light of Amy Richlin's *The Garden of Priapus*

(New Haven 1983). There is no reason to believe that his attitudes diverge substantially from the social traditions of the day; certainly they do not from its literary postures.

Richlin points out that in erotic poetry the world is divided between the beloved and the poet/lover. The object of affection has no existence whatever outside of the epigram and so, as the embodiment of an ideal, can be assigned a shifting and ill-defined identity. There are two positive objects of sexuality: the ἑταίρα, the mistress; and the ἐρόμενος, the beloved boy. No address is made in these epigrams to women of higher social status, to married women, or to adult males. Most of Meleager's epigrams, although not all of them, avoid precise physical details and speak in idealized generalities. The boys especially are described as golden adolescents, who live and play in a timeless existence with no future; they are simply romantic objects, ideal visions, and, in all likelihood, reflections of a literary tradition as are the poet's sentiments towards women, whose status is either that of ἑταίραι or of prostitutes. The ideal mistress appears to be physically and emotionally distant. As Meleager invokes puberty against recalcitrant boys, he invokes wrinkles, drooping breasts, and old age for an uncooperative mistress, and hurls vituperation against a strumpet well past her prime (Selection 60: *A. P.* 5. 204).

Whether it be for boys or mistresses, the poet/lover often abases himself:

Κεῖμαι· λὰξ ἐπίβαινε κατ᾽ αὐχένος, ἄγριε δαῖμον·
(Selection 16: *A. P.* 12. 48. 1)

Aside from the gifts which he proffers, the lover fails to suggest his good features with which he might promote his interests and obtain his beloved's favor. On the other hand, we must remember that the poet is creator as well as the dominant male figure and is, for all intents and purposes, therefore omnipotent.

Meleager's language ranges from passages of high elaboration to those of utmost simplicity, and is distinguised by its ease and lack of painful mannerism. He has a distinct gift for the generation of compound words (whether adjectives and verbs) which contribute to the lucidity and concision of his verse. His poetry carefully blends traditional elements and conventional formulas with original and startling expressions such as a description of the eyes as "boy-hunting hounds" (Selection 106: *A. P.* 12. 92. 1).

Some critics have attempted to identify Syrian influence in his poetry and to suggest that his epigrams show the effects of Asiaticism. Such fine points of style are elusive after 2,000 years and their detection quite subjective. It is perhaps safer to observe simply that Greek literary practices were constantly and inevitably modified in some aspects and expanded in others through frequent contact with non-Greek cultural forces and, expectably, through idiosyncratic artistic impulses.

Although Swinburne spoke in terms of Meleager's "iostephanous and tawdry Muse," the poet has had numerous admirers and English translators within the last one hundred years. Specific mention should be made of W. R. Paton (*The Greek Anthology* [Cambridge, MA 1916]), Richard Aldington's translation of 128 epigrams (*The Poems of Meleager of Gadara* [London 1920]), and the homage to Meleager of Aldington's quondam wife, Hilda Doolittle:

> He said:
> "I shall make her a wreath;"
> he said:
> "I will write it thus:
> I will bring the lily that laughs,
> I will twine
> with soft narcissus, the myrtle,
> sweet crocus, white violet,
> the purple hyacinth, and last,
> the rose, loved-of-all
> that they may drip on your hair
> the less soft flowers,
> may mingle sweet with the sweet
> of Heliodora's locks,
> myrrh-curled.
> I saw him out the door,
> I thought:
> there will never be a poet
> in all the centuries after this,
> who will dare to write,
> after my friend's verse,

Meleager

> "a girl's mouth
> is a lily kissed."
>
> (from *Heliodora*)

Those interested in the quixotic Baron Frederick Corvo (Frederick Rolfe) should refer to the recent facsimile edition of his translations of Meleager, edited by Ian Fletcher and John Stokes (*The Songs of Meleager* [New York and London 1984]). Finally, worthy of attention are the versions of Walter Headlam (*Fifty Poems of Meleager* [London 1890]) and the verse translations of Peter Whigham accompanied by the prose renditions of Peter Jay in *The Poems of Meleager* (Berkeley and Los Angeles 1975).

1

Μοῦσα φίλα, τίνι τάνδε φέρεις πάγκαρπον ἀοιδάν,
    ἢ τίς ὁ καὶ τεύξας ὑμνοθετᾶν στέφανον;
ἄνυσε μὲν Μελέαγρος, ἀριζάλῳ δὲ Διοκλεῖ
    μναμόσυνον ταύταν ἐξεπόνησε χάριν,
5 πολλὰ μὲν ἐμπλέξας Ἀνύτης κρίνα, πολλὰ δὲ Μοιροῦς
    λείρια, καὶ Σαπφοῦς βαιὰ μὲν ἀλλὰ ῥόδα,
νάρκισσόν τε τορῶν Μελανιππίδου ἔγκυον ὕμνων,
    καὶ νέον οἰνάνθης κλῆμα Σιμωνίδεω,
σὺν δ' ἀναμὶξ πλέξας μυρόπνουν εὐάνθεμον ἶριν
10   Νοσσίδος, ἧς δέλτοις κηρὸν ἔτηξεν Ἔρως·
τῇ δ' ἅμα καὶ σάμψυχον ἀφ' ἡδυπνόοιο Ῥιανοῦ,
    καὶ γλυκὺν Ἠρίννης παρθενόχρωτα κρόκον,
Ἀλκαίου τε λάληθρον ἐν ὑμνοπόλοις ὑάκινθον,
    καὶ Σαμίου δάφνης κλῶνα μελαμπέταλον.
15 ἐν δὲ Λεωνίδεω θαλεροὺς κισσοῖο κορύμβους,
    Μνασάλκου τε κόμας ὀξυτόρου πίτυος,
†βλαισήν τε πλατάνιστον ἀπέθρισε Παμφίλου οἴνης†
    σύμπλεκτον καρύης ἔρνεσι Παγκράτεος,
Τύμνεώ τ' εὐπέταλον λεύκην, χλοερόν τε σίσυμβρον
20   Νικίου, Εὐφήμου τ' ἀμμότροφον πάραλον·
ἐν δ' ἄρα Δαμάγητον, ἴον μέλαν, ἡδύ τε μύρτον
    Καλλιμάχου στυφελοῦ μεστὸν ἀεὶ μέλιτος,
λυχνίδα τ' Εὐφορίωνος, ἰδ' †ἐν Μούσησιν ἄμεινον†,
    ὃς Διὸς ἐκ κούρων ἔσχεν ἐπωνυμίην.
25 τῇσι δ' ἄμ' Ἡγήσιππον ἐνέπλεκε, μαινάδα βότρυν,
    Πέρσου τ' εὐώδη σχοῖνον ἀμησάμενος,
σὺν δ' ἅμα καὶ γλυκύμηλον ἀπ' ἀκρεμόνων Διοτίμου,
    καὶ ῥοιῆς ἄνθη πρῶτα Μενεκράτεος,
μυρραίους τε κλάδους Νικαινέτου, ἠδὲ Φαέννου
30   τέρμινθον, βλωθρήν τ' ἀχράδα Σιμίεω·
ἐν δὲ καὶ ἐκ λειμῶνος ἀμωμήτοιο σέλινα
    βαιὰ διακνίζων ἄνθεα Παρθενίδος,
λείψανά τ' εὐκαρπεῦντα μελιστάκτων ἀπὸ Μουσέων
    ξανθοὺς ἐκ καλάμης Βακχυλίδεω στάχυας,
35 ἐν δ' ἄρ' Ἀνακρείοντα, τὸ μὲν γλυκὺ κεῖνο μέλισμα
    νέκταρος, εἰς δ' ἐλέγους ἄσπορον ἀνθέμιον,

ἐν δὲ καὶ ἐκ φορβῆς σκολιότριχος ἄνθος ἀκάνθης
      Ἀρχιλόχου, μικρὰς στράγγας ἀπ' ὠκεανοῦ,
τοῖς δ' ἅμ' Ἀλεξάνδροιο νέους ὄρπηκας ἐλαίης,
40   ἠδὲ Πολυκλείτου πορφυρέην κύαμον.
ἐν δ' ἄρ' ἀμάρακον ἧκε, Πολυστράτου ἄνθος ἀοιδῶν,
      Φοίνισσάν τε νέην κύπρον ἀπ' Ἀντιπάτρου.
καὶ μὴν καὶ Συρίαν σταχυότριχα θήκατο νάρδον,
      ὑμνοθέταν Ἑρμοῦ δῶρον ἀειδόμενον,
45 ἐν δὲ Ποσείδιππόν τε καὶ Ἡδύλον, ἄγρι' ἀρούρης,
      Σικελίδεώ τ' ἀνέμοις ἄνθεα φυόμενα.
ναὶ μὴν καὶ χρύσειον ἀεὶ θείοιο Πλάτωνος
      κλῶνα, τὸν ἐξ ἀρετῆς πάντοθι λαμπόμενον,
ἄστρων τ' ἴδριν Ἄρατον ὁμοῦ βάλεν, οὐρανομάκευς
50   φοίνικος κείρας πρωτογόνους ἕλικας,
λωτόν τ' εὐχαίτην Χαιρήμονος, ἐν φλογὶ μίξας
      Φαιδίμου, Ἀνταγόρου τ' εὔστροφον ὄμμα βοός,
τάν τε φιλάκρητον Θεοδωρίδεω νεοθαλῆ
      ἕρπυλλον, κυάνων τ' ἄνθεα Φανίεω,
55 ἄλλων τ' ἔρνεα πολλὰ νεόγραφα, τοῖς δ' ἅμα Μούσης
      καὶ σφετέρης ἔτι που πρώιμα λευκόια.
ἀλλὰ φίλοις μὲν ἐμοῖσι φέρω χάριν· ἔστι δὲ μύσταις
      κοινὸς ὁ τῶν Μουσέων ἡδυεπὴς στέφανος.

2

Νᾶσος ἐμὰ θρέπτειρα Τύρος, πάτρα δέ με τεκνοῖ
      Ἀτθὶς ἐν Ἀσσυρίοις ναιομένα Γάδαρα,
Εὐκράτεω δ' ἔβλαστον ὁ σὺν Μούσαις Μελέαγρος
      πρῶτα Μενιππείοις συντροχάσας Χάρισιν.
5 εἰ δὲ Σύρος, τί τὸ θαῦμα; μίαν, ξένε, πατρίδα κόσμον
      ναίομεν, ἓν θνατοὺς πάντας ἔτικτε Χάος.
πουλυετὴς δ' ἐχάραξα τάδ' ἐν δέλτοισι πρὸ τύμβου·
      γήρως γὰρ γείτων ἐγγύθεν Ἀίδεω.
ἀλλά με τὸν λαλιὸν καὶ πρεσβύτην πάρος εἰπών
10   χαίρειν εἰς γῆρας καὐτὸς ἵκοιο λάλον.

3

Πρώτα μοι Γαδάρων κλεινὰ πόλις ἔπλετο πάτρα,
    ἤνδρωσεν δ᾽ ἱερὰ δεξαμένα με Τύρος·
εἰς γῆρας δ᾽ ὅτ᾽ ἔβην, <ἅ> καὶ Δία θρεψαμένα Κῶς
    κἀμὲ θετὸν Μερόπων ἀστὸν ἐγηροτρόφει·
5 Μοῦσαι δ᾽ εἰν ὀλίγοις με τὸν Εὐκράτεω Μελέαγρον
    παῖδα Μενιππείοις ἠγλάισαν Χάρισιν.

4

᾽Ατρέμας, ὦ ξένε, βαῖνε· παρ᾽ εὐσεβέσιν γὰρ ὁ πρέσβυς
    εὕδει κοιμηθεὶς ὕπνον ὀφειλόμενον
Εὐκράτεω Μελέαγρος, ὁ τὸν γλυκύδακρυν Ἔρωτα
    καὶ Μούσας ἱλαραῖς συστολίσας χάρισιν·
5 ὃν θεόπαις ἤνδρωσε Τύρος Γαδάρων θ᾽ ἱερὰ χθών,
    Κῶς δ᾽ ἐρατὴ Μερόπων πρέσβυν ἐγηροτρόφει.
ἀλλ᾽ εἰ μὲν Σύρος ἐσσί, σαλάμ· εἰ δ᾽ οὖν σύ γε Φοῖνιξ,
    ναίδιος· εἰ δ᾽ Ἕλλην, χαῖρε· τὸ δ᾽ αὐτὸ φράσον.

5

Πτανέ, τί σοὶ σιβύνας, τί δὲ καὶ συὸς εὖαδε δέρμα,
    καὶ τίς ἐὼν στάλας σύμβολόν ἐσσι τίνος;
οὐ γὰρ Ἔρωτ᾽ ἐνέπω σε· τί γάρ, νεκύεσσι πάροικος
    Ἵμερος; αἰάζειν ὁ θρασὺς οὐκ ἔμαθεν·
5 οὐδὲ μὲν οὐδ᾽ αὐτὸν ταχύπουν Χρόνον· ἔμπαλι γὰρ δή
    κεῖνος μὲν τριγέρων, σοὶ δὲ τέθηλε μέλη.
ἀλλ᾽ ἄρα, ναί, δοκέω γάρ, ὁ γᾶς ὑπένερθε σοφιστάς
    ἐστί, σὺ δ᾽ ὁ πτερόεις τοὔνομα τοῦδε λόγος.
Λατῴας δ᾽ ἄμφηκες ἔχεις γέρας ἔς τε γέλωτα
10   καὶ σπουδὰν καί που μέτρον ἐρωτογράφον.
ναὶ μὲν δὴ Μελέαγρον ὁμώνυμον Οἰνέος υἱῷ
    σύμβολα σημαίνει ταῦτα συοκτασίας.
χαῖρε καὶ ἐν φθιμένοισιν, ἐπεὶ καὶ Μοῦσαν Ἔρωτι
    καὶ Χάριτας σοφίαν εἰς μίαν ἡρμόσαο.

6

Δεινὸς Ἔρως, δεινός· τί δὲ τὸ πλέον ἢν πάλιν εἴπω
  καὶ πάλιν οἰμώζων πολλάκι, 'δεινὸς Ἔρως';
ἦ γὰρ ὁ παῖς τούτοισι γελᾷ καὶ πυκνὰ κακισθεὶς
  ἥδεται, ἢν δ' εἴπω λοίδορα, καὶ τρέφεται.
5 θαῦμα δέ μοι πῶς ἆρα διὰ γλαυκοῖο φανεῖσα
  κύματος, ἐξ ὑγροῦ, Κύπρι, σὺ πῦρ τέτοκας.

7

Ναὶ τὰν Κύπριν, Ἔρως, φλέξω τὰ σὰ πάντα πυρώσας
  τόξα τε καὶ Σκυθικὴν ἰοδόκον φαρέτρην.
φλέξω ναί· τί μάταια γελᾷς καὶ σιμὰ σεσηρὼς
  μυχθίζεις; τάχα που σαρδάνιον γελάσεις.
5 ἦ γάρ σευ τὰ ποδηγὰ Πόθων ὠκύπτερα κόψας
  χαλκόδετον σφίγξω σοῖς περὶ ποσσὶ πέδην.
καίτοι Καδμεῖον κράτος οἴσομεν εἴ σε πάροικον
  ψυχῇ συζεύξω, λύγκα παρ' αἰπολίοις.
ἀλλ' ἴθι, δυσνίκητε, λαβὼν δ' ἔπι κοῦφα πέδιλα
10 ἐκπέτασον ταχινὰς εἰς ἑτέρους πτέρυγας.

8

Τί ξένον εἰ βροτολοιγὸς Ἔρως τὰ πυρίπνοα τόξα
  βάλλει καὶ λαμυροῖς ὄμμασι πικρὰ γελᾷ;
οὐ μάτηρ στέργει μὲν Ἄρη, γαμέτις δὲ τέτυκται
  Ἀφαίστου, κοινὰ καὶ πυρὶ καὶ ξίφεσι;
5 ματρὸς δ' οὐ μάτηρ ἀνέμων μάστιξι Θάλασσα
  τραχὺ βοᾷ; γενέτας δ' οὔτε τις οὔτε τινός.
τοὔνεκεν Ἀφαίστου μὲν ἔχει φλόγα, κύμασι δ' ὀργάν
  στέρξεν ἴσαν, Ἄρεως δ' αἱματόφυρτα βέλη.

9

Οὔ μοι παιδομανής κραδία· τί δὲ τερπνόν, Ἔρωτες,
    ἀνδροβατεῖν εἰ μὴ δούς τι λαβεῖν ἐθέλοι;
ἁ χεὶρ γὰρ τὰν χεῖρα· †καλα μεν ειν παρακοιτις
    ειν† πᾶς ἄρσην ἀρσενικαῖς λαβίσιν.

10

Αἰεί μοι δύνει μὲν ἐν οὔασιν ἦχος Ἔρωτος,
    ὄμμα δὲ σῖγα Πόθοις τὸ γλυκὺ δάκρυ φέρει·
οὐδ' ἡ νύξ, οὐ φέγγος ἐκοίμισεν, ἀλλ' ὑπὸ φίλτρων
    ἤδη που κραδίᾳ γνωστὸς ἔνεστι τύπος.
5   ὦ πτανοί, μὴ καί ποτ' ἐφίπτασθαι μέν, Ἔρωτες,
    οἴδατ' ἀποπτῆναι δ' οὐδ' ὅσον ἰσχύετε;

11

Ἄνθεμά σοι Μελέαγρος ἑὸν συμπαίστορα λύχνον,
    Κύπρι φίλη, μύστην σῶν θέτο παννυχίδων.

12

Ἀκρίς, ἐμῶν ἀπάτημα πόθων, παραμύθιον ὕπνου,
    ἀκρίς, ἀρουραίη Μοῦσα λιγυπτέρυγε,
αὐτοφυὲς μίμημα λύρας, κρέκε μοί τι ποθεινόν
    ἐγκρούουσα φίλοις ποσσὶ λάλους πτέρυγας,
5   ὥς με πόνων ῥύσαιο παναγρύπνοιο μερίμνης,
    ἀκρί, μιτωσαμένη φθόγγον ἐρωτοπλάνον·
δῶρα δέ σοι γήτειον ἀειθαλὲς ὀρθρινὰ δώσω
    καὶ δροσερὰς στόμασι σχιζομένοις ψακάδας.

13

Ἀχήεις τέττιξ, δροσεραῖς σταγόνεσσι μεθυσθείς
    ἀγρονόμαν μέλπεις μοῦσαν ἐρημολάλον,
ἄκρα δ' ἐφεζόμενος πετάλοις πριονώδεσι κώλοις
    αἰθίοπι κλάζεις χρωτὶ μέλισμα λύρας·

5 ἀλλά, φίλος, φθέγγου τι νέον δενδρώδεσι Νύμφαις
  παίγνιον, ἀντῳδὸν Πανὶ κρέκων κέλαδον,
ὄφρα φυγὼν τὸν Ἔρωτα μεσημβρινὸν ὕπνον ἀγρεύσω
  ἐνθάδ’ ὑπὸ σκιερᾷ κεκλιμένος πλατάνῳ.

14

Τήν περινηχομένην ψυχὴν ἂν πολλάκι καίῃς,
  φεύξετ’, Ἔρως· καὐτή, σχέτλι’, ἔχει πτέρυγας.

15

Ματρὸς ἔτ’ ἐν κόλποισιν ὁ νήπιος ὀρθρινὰ παίζων
  ἀστραγάλοις τοὐμὸν πνεῦμ’ ἐκύβευσεν Ἔρως.

16

Κεῖμαι· λὰξ ἐπίβαινε κατ’ αὐχένος, ἄγριε δαῖμον·
  οἶδά σε, ναὶ μὰ θεούς, καὶ βαρὺν ὄντα φέρειν·
οἶδα καὶ ἔμπυρα τόξα· βαλὼν δ’ ἐπ’ ἐμὴν φρένα πυρσούς
  οὐ φλέξεις· ἤδη πᾶσα γάρ ἐστι τέφρη.

17

Ψυχὴ δυσδάκρυτε, τί σοι τὸ πεπανθὲν Ἔρωτος
  τραῦμα διὰ σπλάγχνων αὖθις ἀναφλέγεται;
μὴ μὴ πρός σε Διός, μὴ πρὸς Διός, ὦ φιλάβουλε,
  κινήσῃς τέφρῃ πῦρ ὑπολαμπόμενον.
5 αὐτίκα γάρ, λήθαργε κακῶν, πάλιν εἴ σε φυγοῦσαν
  λήψετ’ Ἔρως, εὑρὼν δραπέτιν αἰκίσεται.

18

Ἁ Κύπρις θήλεια γυναικομανῆ φλόγα βάλλει,
  ἄρσενα δ’ αὐτὸς Ἔρως ἵμερον ἀνιοχεῖ.
ποῖ ῥέψω; ποτὶ παῖδ’ ἢ ματέρα; φαμὶ δὲ καὐτάν
  Κύπριν ἐρεῖν, ‘νικᾷ τὸ θρασὺ παιδάριον’.

18

19

Βεβλήσθω κύβος· ἅπτε· πορεύσομαι.—Ἠνίδε τόλμαν·
οἰνοβαρές, τίν' ἔχεις φροντίδα;—Κωμάσομαι,
κωμάσομαι.—Ποῖ, θυμέ, τρέπῃ;—Τί δ' Ἔρωτι λογισμός;
ἅπτε τάχος.—Ποῦ δ' ἡ πρόσθε λόγων μελέτη;
5 —Ἐρρίφθω σοφίας ὁ πολὺς πόνος· ἓν μόνον οἶδα
τουθ', ὅτι καὶ Ζηνὸς λῆμα καθεῖλεν Ἔρως.

20

Οἴσω ναὶ μὰ σέ, Βάκχε, τὸ σὸν θράσος· ἀγέο κώμων,
ἄρχε, θεὸς θνατὰν ἀνιόχει κραδίαν.
ἐν πυρὶ γενναθεὶς στέργεις φλόγα τὰν ἐν Ἔρωτι
καί με πάλιν δήσας τὸν σὸν ἄγεις ἱκέταν.
5 ἦ προδότας κἄπιστος ἔφυς, τεὰ δ' ὄργια κρύπτειν
αὐδῶν, ἐκφαίνειν τἀμὰ σὺ νῦν ἐθέλεις.

21

Οὔ σοι ταῦτ' ἐβόων, ψυχή, 'ναὶ Κύπριν ἁλώσει,
ὦ δύσερως, ἰξῷ πυκνὰ προσιπταμένη';
οὐκ ἐβόων; εἷλέν σε πάγη· τί μάτην ἐνὶ δεσμοῖς
σπαίρεις; αὐτὸς Ἔρως τὰ πτερά σου δέδεκεν,
5 καί σ' ἐπὶ πῦρ ἔστησε, μύροις δ' ἔρρανε λιπόπνουν,
δῶκε δὲ διψώσῃ δάκρυα θερμὰ πιεῖν.

22

Ἆ ψυχὴ βαρύμοχθε, σὺ δ' ἄρτι μὲν ἐκ πυρὸς αἴθῃ,
ἄρτι δ' ἀναψύχεις πνεῦμ' ἀναλεξαμένη.
τί κλαίεις; τὸν ἄτεγκτον ὅτ' ἐν κόλποισιν Ἔρωτα
ἔτρεφες, οὐκ ᾔδεις ὡς ἐπὶ σοὶ τρέφετο;
5 οὐκ ᾔδεις; νῦν γνῶθι καλῶν ἄλλαγμα τροφείων
πῦρ ἅμα καὶ ψυχρὰν δεξαμένη χιόνα.
αὐτὴ ταῦθ' εἵλου· φέρε τὸν πόνον· ἄξια πάσχεις
ὧν ἔδρας ὀπτῷ καιομένη μέλιτι.

23

Ναὶ μὰ τὸν εὐπλόκαμον Τιμοῦς φιλέρωτα κίκιννον,
        ναὶ μυρόπνουν Δημοῦς χρῶτα τὸν ὑπναπάτην,
ναὶ πάλιν Ἰλιάδος φίλα παίγνια, ναὶ φιλάγρυπνον
        λύχνον ἐμῶν κώμων πόλλ' ἐπιδόντα τέλη·
5   βαιὸν ἔχω τό γε λειφθέν, Ἔρως, ἐπὶ χείλεσι πνεῦμα·
        εἰ δ' ἐθέλεις καὶ τοῦτ', εἰπὲ καὶ ἐκπτύσομαι.

24

Οὐ πλόκαμον Τιμοῦς, οὐ σάνδαλον Ἡλιοδώρας,
        οὐ τὸ μυρόρραντον Δημαρίου πρόθυρον,
οὐ τρυφερὸν μείδημα βοώπιδος Ἀντικλείας,
        οὐ τοὺς ἀρτιθαλεῖς Δωροθέας στεφάνους,
5   οὐκέτι σοὶ φαρέτρη <   > πτερόεντας ὀιστοὺς
        κρύπτει, Ἔρως· ἐν ἐμοὶ πάντα γάρ ἐστι βέλη.

25

Ἁ φίλερως χαροποῖς Ἀσκληπιὰς οἷα Γαλήνης
        ὄμμασι συμπείθει πάντας ἐρωτοπλοεῖν.

26

Δημὼ λευκοπάρειε, σὲ μέν τις ἔχων ὑπόχρωτα
        τέρπεται, ἁ δ' ἐν ἐμοὶ νῦν στενάχει κραδία.
εἰ δέ σε σαββατικὸς κατέχει πόθος, οὐ μέγα θαῦμα·
        ἐστὶ καὶ ἐν ψυχροῖς σάββασι θερμὸς Ἔρως.

27

Ὄρθρε τί μοι δυσέραστε ταχὺς περὶ κοῖτον ἐπέστης
        ἄρτι φίλας Δημοῦς χρωτὶ χλιαινομένῳ;
εἴθε πάλιν στρέψας ταχινὸν δρόμον Ἕσπερος εἴης,
        ὦ γλυκὺ φῶς βάλλων εἰς ἐμὲ πικρότατον.
5   ἤδη γὰρ καὶ πρόσθεν ἐπ' Ἀλκμήνην Διὸς ἦλθες
        ἀντίος· οὐκ ἀδαής ἐσσι παλινδρομίης.

28

Ὄρθρε, τί νῦν, δυσέραστε, βραδὺς περὶ κόσμον ἑλίσσῃ
    ἄλλος ἐπεὶ Δημοῦς θάλπεθ' ὑπὸ χλανίδι;
ἀλλ' ὅτε τὰν ῥαδινὰν κόλποις ἔχον, ὠκὺς ἐπέστης
    ὡς βάλλων ἐπ' ἐμοὶ φῶς ἐπιχαιρέκακον.

29

Ἀδὺ μέλος, ναὶ Πᾶνα τὸν Ἀρκάδα, πηκτίδι μέλπεις,
    Ζηνοφίλα, ναὶ Πᾶν', ἁδὺ κρέκεις τι μέλος.
ποῖ σε φύγω; πάντη με περιστείχουσιν Ἔρωτες,
    οὐδ' ὅσον ἀμπνεῦσαι βαιὸν ἐῶσι χρόνον.
5 ἢ γάρ μοι μορφὰ βάλλει πόθον ἢ πάλι μοῦσα
    ἢ χάρις ἢ—τί λέγω; πάντα· πυρὶ φλέγομαι.

30

Ἡδυμελεῖς Μοῦσαι σὺν πηκτίδι καὶ Λόγος ἔμφρων
    σὺν πειθοῖ καὶ Ἔρως κάλλος ὑφηνιοχῶν,
Ζηνοφίλα, σοὶ σκῆπτρα Πόθων ἀπένειμαν, ἐπεί σοι
    αἱ τρισσαὶ Χάριτες τρεῖς ἔδοσαν χάριτας.

31

Ἤδη λευκόιον θάλλει, θάλλει δὲ φίλομβρος
    νάρκισσος, θάλλει δ' οὐρεσίφοιτα κρίνα·
ἤδη δ' ἡ φιλέραστος, ἐν ἄνθεσιν ὥριμον ἄνθος,
    Ζηνοφίλα Πειθοῦς ἡδὺ τέθηλε ῥόδον.
5 λειμῶνες, τί μάταια κόμαις ἔπι φαιδρὰ γελᾶτε;
    ἁ γὰρ παῖς κρέσσων ἁδυπνόων στεφάνων.

32

Τίς μοι Ζηνοφίλαν λαλιὰν παρέδειξεν ἑταίραν;
    τίς μίαν ἐκ τρισσῶν ἤγαγέ μοι Χάριτα;
ἦ ῥ' ἐτύμως ἀνὴρ κεχαρισμένον ἄνυσεν ἔργον
    δῶρα διδοὺς καὐτὰν τὰν Χάριν ἐν χάριτι.

33

Ὀξυβόαι κώνωπες, ἀναιδέες, αἵματος ἀνδρῶν
    σίφωνες, νυκτὸς κνώδαλα διπτέρυγα,
βαιὸν Ζηνοφίλαν, λίτομαι, πάρεθ' ἥσυχον ὕπνῳ
    εὕδειν, τἀμὰ δ', ἰδού, σαρκοφαγεῖτε μέλη.
5 καίτοι πρὸς τί μάτην αὐδῶ; καὶ θῆρες ἄτεγκτοι
    τέρπονται τρυφερῷ χρωτὶ χλιαινόμενοι.
ἀλλ' ἔτι νῦν προλέγω, κακὰ θρέμματα λήγετε τόλμης,
    ἢ γνώσεσθε χερῶν ζηλοτύπων δύναμιν.

34

Πταίης μοι κώνωψ ταχὺς ἄγγελος, οὔασι δ' ἄκροις
    Ζηνοφίλας ψαύσας προσψιθύριζε τάδε·
'ἄγρυπνος μίμνει σε, σὺ δ' ὦ λήθαργε φιλούντων
    εὕδεις'. εἶα πέτευ, ναὶ φιλόμουσε πέτευ·
5 ἥσυχα δὲ φθέγξαι, μὴ καὶ σύγκοιτον ἐγείρας
    κινήσῃς ἐπ' ἐμοὶ ζηλοτύπους ὀδύνας.
ἢν δ' ἀγάγῃς τὴν παῖδα, δορᾷ στέψω σε λέοντος,
    κώνωψ, καὶ δώσω χειρὶ φέρειν ῥόπαλον.

35

Τὸ σκύφος ἡδὺ γέγηθε, λέγει δ' ὅτι τᾶς φιλέρωτος
    Ζηνοφίλας ψαύει τοῦ λαλιοῦ στόματος·
ὄλβιον· εἴθ' ὑπ' ἐμοῖς νῦν χείλεσι χείλεα θεῖσα
    ἀπνευστὶ ψυχὰν τὰν ἐν ἐμοὶ προπίοι.

36

Εὕδεις, Ζηνοφίλα, τρυφερὸν θάλος· εἴθ' ἐπὶ σοὶ νῦν
    ἄπτερος εἰσήειν ὕπνος ἐπὶ βλεφάροις,
ὡς ἐπὶ σοὶ μηδ' οὗτος ὁ καὶ Διὸς ὄμματα θέλγων
    φοιτήσαι, κάτεχον δ' αὐτὸς ἐγώ σε μόνος.

37

Κηρύσσω τὸν Ἔρωτα τὸν ἄγριον· ἄρτι γὰρ ἄρτι
    ὀρθρινὸς ἐκ κοίτας ᾤχετ' ἀποπτάμενος.
ἐστὶ δ' ὁ παῖς γλυκύδακρυς, ἀείλαλος, ὠκύς, ἀθαμβής,
    σιμὰ γελῶν, πτερόεις νῶτα, φαρετροφόρος.
5   πατρὸς δ' οὐκέτ' ἔχω φράζειν τίνος· οὔτε γὰρ αἰθήρ
    οὐ χθών φησι τεκεῖν τὸν θρασύν, οὐ πέλαγος·
πάντῃ γὰρ καὶ πᾶσιν ἀπέχθεται· ἀλλ' ἐσορᾶτε
    μή που νῦν ψυχαῖς ἄλλα τίθησι λίνα.
καίτοι κεῖνος, ἰδού, περὶ φωλεόν· οὔ με λέληθας,
10   τοξότα, Ζηνοφίλας ὄμμασι κρυπτόμενος.

38

Πωλείσθω καὶ ματρὸς ἔτ' ἐν κόλποισι καθεύδων,
    πωλείσθω· τί δέ μοι τὸ θρασὺ τοῦτο τρέφειν;
καὶ γὰρ σιμὸν ἔφυ καὶ ὑπόπτερον, ἄκρα δ' ὄνυξιν
    κνίζει, καὶ κλαῖον πολλὰ μεταξὺ γελᾷ.
5   πρὸς δ' ἔτι λοιπὸν ἄθρεπτον ἀείλαλον ὀξὺ δεδορκός
    ἄγριον, οὐδ' αὐτᾷ ματρὶ φίλα τιθασόν.
πάντα τέρας· τοιγὰρ πεπράσεται· εἴ τις ἀπόπλους
    ἔμπορος ὠνεῖσθαι παῖδα θέλει, προσίτω.
καίτοι λίσσετ', ἰδού, δεδακρυμένος· οὔ σ' ἔτι πωλῶ·
10   θάρσει· Ζηνοφίλᾳ σύντροφος ὧδε μένε.

39

Αἱ τρισσαὶ Χάριτες τρισσὸν στεφάνωμα συνεῖραν
    Ζηνοφίλᾳ τρισσᾶς σύμβολα καλλοσύνας·
ἁ μὲν ἐπὶ χρωτὸς θεμένα πόθον, ἁ δ' ἐπὶ μορφᾶς
    ἵμερον, ἁ δὲ λόγοις τὸ γλυκύμυθον ἔπος.
5   τρισσάκις εὐδαίμων, ἇς καὶ Κύπρις ὤπλισεν εὐνάν
    καὶ Πειθὼ μύθους καὶ γλυκὺ κάλλος Ἔρως.

40

Ζηνοφίλᾳ κάλλος μὲν Ἔρως σύγκοιτα δὲ φίλτρα
    Κύπρις ἔδωκεν ἔχειν, αἱ Χάριτες δὲ χάριν.

41

Ψυχή μοι προλέγει φεύγειν πόθον Ἡλιοδώρας
    δάκρυα καὶ ζήλους τοὺς πρὶν ἐπισταμένη.
φησὶ μέν, ἀλλὰ φυγεῖν οὔ μοι σθένος· ἡ γὰρ ἀναιδής
    αὐτὴ καὶ προλέγει καὶ προλέγουσα φιλεῖ.

42

Ἔγχει καὶ πάλιν εἰπέ, πάλιν πάλιν, Ἡλιοδώρας·
    εἰπέ, σὺν ἀκρήτῳ τὸ γλυκὺ μίσγ' ὄνομα.
καί μοι τὸν βρεχθέντα μύροις καὶ χθιζὸν ἐόντα
    μναμόσυνον κείνας ἀμφιτίθει στέφανον.
5 δακρύει φιλέραστον, ἰδού, ῥόδον, οὕνεκα κείναν
    ἄλλοθι κοὐ κόλποις ἡμετέροις ἐσορᾷ.

43

Ἔγχει τᾶς Πειθοῦς καὶ Κύπριδος Ἡλιοδώρας
    καὶ πάλι τᾶς αὐτᾶς ἀδυλόγου Χάριτος·
αὐτὰ γὰρ μί' ἐμοὶ γράφεται θεός, ἇς τὸ ποθεινόν
    οὔνομ' ἐν ἀκρήτῳ συγκεράσας πίομαι.

44

Ναὶ τὸν Ἔρωτα θέλω τὸ παρ' οὔασιν Ἡλιοδώρας
    φθέγμα κλύειν ἢ τᾶς Λατοΐδεω κιθάρας.

45

Ὁ στέφανος περὶ κρατὶ μαραίνεται Ἡλιοδώρας,
    αὐτὴ δ' ἐκλάμπει τοῦ στεφάνου στέφανος.

46

Πλέξω λευκόιον, πλέξω δ᾽ ἁπαλὴν ἅμα μύρτοις
    νάρκισσον, πλέξω καὶ τὰ γελῶντα κρίνα,
πλέξω καὶ κρόκον ἡδύν, ἐπιπλέξω δ᾽ ὑάκινθον
    πορφυρέην, πλέξω καὶ φιλέραστα ῥόδα,
5 ὡς ἂν ἐπὶ κροτάφοις μυροβοστρύχου Ἡλιοδώρας
    εὐπλόκαμον χαίτην ἀνθοβολῇ στέφανος.

47

Φαμί ποτ᾽ ἐν μύθοις τὰν εὔλαλον Ἡλιοδώραν
    νικάσειν αὐτὰς τὰς Χάριτας χάρισιν.

48

Ἐντὸς ἐμῆς κραδίης τὴν εὔλαλον Ἡλιοδώραν
    ψυχὴν τῆς ψυχῆς ἔπλασεν αὐτὸς Ἔρως.

49

Τρηχὺς ὄνυξ, ὑπ᾽ Ἔρωτος ἀνέτραφες Ἡλιοδώρας·
    ταύτης γὰρ δύνει κνίσμα καὶ ἐς κραδίην.

50

Ἀνθοδίαιτε μέλισσα, τί μοι χροὸς Ἡλιοδώρας
    ψαύεις ἐκπρολιποῦσ᾽ εἰαρινὰς κάλυκας;
ἦ σύ γε μηνύεις ὅτι καὶ γλυκὺ καὶ †δύσοιστον†
    πικρὸν ἀεὶ κραδίᾳ κέντρον Ἔρωτος ἔχει;
5 ναὶ δοκέω τοῦτ᾽ εἶπας· ἰὼ φιλέραστε, παλίμπους
    στεῖχε· πάλαι τὴν σὴν οἴδαμεν ἀγγελίην.

51

Ἓν τόδε, παμμήτειρα θεῶν, λίτομαί σε, φίλη Νύξ,
    ναὶ λίτομαι κώμων σύμπλανε πότνια Νύξ·
εἴ τις ὑπὸ χλαίνῃ βεβλημένος Ἡλιοδώρας
    θάλπεται ὑπναπάτῃ χρωτὶ χλιαινόμενος,
5 κοιμάσθω μὲν λύχνος, ὁ δ᾽ ἐν κόλποισιν ἐκείνης
    ῥιπτασθεὶς κείσθω δεύτερος Ἐνδυμίων.

52

Ὦ Νύξ, ὦ φιλάγρυπνος ἐμοὶ πόθος Ἡλιοδώρας
    καὶ †σκολιῶν ὄρθρων† κνίσματα δακρυχαρῆ,
ἆρα μένει στοργῆς ἐμὰ λείψανα, καί τι φίλημα
    μνημόσυνον ψυχρᾷ θάλπετ᾽ ἐν εἰκασίᾳ;
5 ἆρα γ᾽ ἔχει σύγκοιτα τὰ δάκρυα, κἀμὸν ὄνειρον
    ψυχαπάτην στέρνοις ἀμφιβαλοῦσα φιλεῖ;
ἢ νέος ἄλλος ἔρως, νέα παίγνια; μήποτε, λύχνε,
    ταῦτ᾽ ἐσίδῃς, εἴης δ᾽ ἧς παρέδωκα φύλαξ.

53

Σφαιριστὰν τὸν Ἔρωτα τρέφω· σοὶ δ᾽, Ἡλιοδώρα,
    βάλλει τὰν ἐν ἐμοὶ παλλομέναν κραδίαν.
ἀλλ᾽ ἄγε συμπαίκταν δέξαι Πόθον· εἰ δ᾽ ἀπὸ σεῦ με
    ῥίψαις, οὐκ οἴσει τὰν ἀπάλαιστρον ὕβριν.

54

Λίσσομ᾽, Ἔρως, τὸν ἄγρυπνον ἐμοὶ πόθον Ἡλιοδώρας
    κοίμισον αἰδεσθεὶς μοῦσαν ἐμὰν ἱκέτιν.
ναὶ γὰρ δὴ τὰ σὰ τόξα, τὰ μὴ δεδιδαγμένα βάλλειν
    ἄλλον, ἀεὶ δ᾽ ἐπ᾽ ἐμοὶ πτανὰ χέοντα βέλη,
5 εἰ καί με κτείναις, λείψω φωνεῦντ᾽ ἐπὶ τύμβῳ
    γράμματ᾽, "Ἔρωτος ὅρα, ξεῖνε, μιαιφονίαν".

55

῞Αρπασται· τίς †τόσσον ἐναιχμᾶσσαι ἄγριος εἶναι†
    τίς τόσος ἀντᾶραι καὶ πρὸς ῎Ερωτα μάχην;
ἅπτε τάχος πεύκας· καίτοι κτύπος· Ἡλιοδώρας·
    βαῖνε πάλιν στέρνων ἐντὸς ἐμῶν, κραδίη.

56

Δάκρυά σοι καὶ νέρθε διὰ χθονός, Ἡλιοδώρα,
    δωροῦμαι, στοργᾶς λείψανον εἰς ᾿Αίδαν,
δάκρυα δυσδάκρυτα· πολυκλαύτῳ δ᾽ ἐπὶ τύμβῳ
    σπένδω μνᾶμα πόθων, μνᾶμα φιλοφροσύνας.
5 οἰκτρὰ γὰρ οἰκτρὰ φίλαν σε καὶ ἐν φθιμένοις Μελέαγρος
    αἰάζω, κενεὰν εἰς ᾿Αχέροντα χάριν.
αἰαῖ ποῦ τὸ ποθεινὸν ἐμοὶ θάλος; ἅρπασεν ῞Αιδας,
    ἅρπασεν, ἀκμαῖον δ᾽ ἄνθος ἔφυρε κόνις.
ἀλλά σε γουνοῦμαι, Γᾶ παντρόφε, τὰν πανόδυρτον
10   ἠρέμα σοῖς κόλποις, μᾶτερ, ἐναγκαλίσαι.

57

Γυμνὴν ἢν ἐσίδῃς Καλλίστιον, ὦ ξένε, φήσεις,
    ‘ἤλλακται διπλοῦν γράμμα Συρηκοσίων’.

58

Εἰπὲ Λυκαινίδι, Δορκάς, ‘ἴδ᾽ ὡς ἐπίτηκτα φιλοῦσα
    ἥλως· οὐ κρύπτει πλαστὸν ἔρωτα χρόνος’.

59

Ἰξὸν ἔχεις τὸ φίλημα, τὰ δ᾽ ὄμματα, Τιμάριον, πῦρ·
    ἢν ἐσίδῃς καίεις, ἢν δὲ θίγῃς δέδεκας.

60

Οὐκέτι Τιμάριον, τὸ πρὶν γλαφυροῖο κέλητος
    πῆγμα, φέρει πλωτὸν Κύπριδος εἰρεσίην·
ἀλλ' ἐπὶ μὲν νώτοισι μετάφρενον ὡς κέρας ἱστῷ
    κυρτοῦται, πολιὸς δ' ἐκλέλυται πρότονος,
5 ἱστία δ' αἰωρητὰ χαλᾷ σπαδονίσματα μαστῶν,
    ἐκ δὲ σάλου στρεπτὰς γαστρὸς ἔχει ῥυτίδας,
νέρθε δὲ πάνθ' ὑπέραντλα νεώς, κοίλη δὲ θάλασσα
    πλημμύρει, γόνασιν δ' ἔντρομός ἐστι σάλος.
δύστανός τις ζωὸς ἔτ' ὢν δ' Ἀχερουσίδα λίμνην
10   πλεύσετ' ἄνωθ' ἐπιβὰς γραὸς ἐπ' εἰκοσόρου.

61

Ὁ τρυφερὸς Διόδωρος ἐς ἠιθέους φλόγα βάλλων
    ἤγρευται λαμυροῖς ὄμμασι Τιμαρίου,
τὸ γλυκύπικρον Ἔρωτος ἔχων βέλος. ἦ τόδε καινόν
    θάμβος ὁρῶ· φλέγεται πῦρ πυρὶ καιόμενον.

62

Καὐτὸς Ἔρως ὁ πτανὸς ἐν αἰθέρι δέσμιος ἥλω
    ἀγρευθεὶς τοῖς σοῖς ὄμμασι, Τιμάριον.

63

Ναὶ τὰν νηξαμέναν χαροποῖς ἐνὶ κύμασι Κύπριν,
    ἐστὶ καὶ ἐκ μορφᾶς ἁ Τρυφέρα τρυφερά.

64

Κῦμα τὸ πικρὸν Ἔρωτος ἀκοίμητοί τε πνέοντες
    ζῆλοι καὶ κώμων χειμέριον πέλαγος,
ποῖ φέρομαι; πάντη δὲ φρενῶν οἴακες ἀφεῖνται·
    ἦ πάλι τὴν τρυφερὴν Σκύλλαν ἐποψόμεθα;

65

Τὸν ταχύπουν ἔτι παῖδα συναρπασθέντα τεκούσης
    ἄρτι μ' ἀπὸ στέρνων οὐατόεντα λαγών
ἐν κόλποις στέργουσα διέτρεφεν ἡ γλυκερόχρως
    Φανίον εἰαρινοῖς ἄνθεσι βοσκόμενον.
5 οὐδέ με μητρὸς ἔτ' εἶχε πόθος, θνήσκω δ' ὑπὸ θοίνης
    ἀπλήστου πολλῇ δαιτὶ παχυνόμενος·
καί μου πρὸς κλισίᾳ κρύψεν νέκυν, ὡς ἐν ὀνείροις
    αἰὲν ὀρᾶν κοίτης γειτονέοντα τάφον.

66

Εὔφορτοι νᾶες πελαγίτιδες, αἳ πόρον Ἕλλης
    πλεῖτε καλὸν κόλποις δεξάμεναι Βορέην,
ἤν που ἐπ' ἠιόνων Κῴαν κατὰ νᾶσον ἴδητε
    Φανίον εἰς χαροπὸν δερκομέναν πέλαγος,
5 τοῦτ' ἔπος ἀγγείλαιτε, καλαὶ νέες, ὥς με κομίζει
    ἵμερος οὐ ναύταν, ποσσὶ δὲ πεζοπόρον·
εἰ γὰρ τοῦτ' εἴποιτ' εὐάγγελοι, αὐτίκα καὶ Ζεύς
    οὔριος ὑμετέρας πνεύσεται εἰς ὀθόνας.

67

Ἔσπευδον τὸν Ἔρωτα φυγεῖν, ὁ δὲ βαιὸν ἀνάψας
    φανίον ἐκ τέφρης εὑρέ με κρυπτόμενον·
κυκλώσας δ' οὐ τόξα, χερὸς δ' ἀκρώνυχα δισσά,
    κνίσμα πυρὸς θραύσας εἷς με λαθὼν ἔβαλεν,
5 ἐκ δὲ φλόγες πάντη μοι ἐπέδραμον· ὦ βραχὺ φέγγος
    λάμψαν ἐμοὶ μέγα πῦρ, Φανίον, ἐν κραδίᾳ.

Meleager

68

Οὔ μ' ἔτρωσεν Ἔρως τόξοις, οὐ λαμπάδ' ἀνάψας
    ὡς πάρος αἰθομένην θῆκεν ὑπὸ κραδίᾳ·
σύγκωμον δὲ Πόθοισι φέρων Κύπριδος μυροφεγγές
    φανίον, ἄκρον ἐμοῖς ὄμμασι πῦρ ἔβαλεν·
5 ἐκ δέ με φέγγος ἔτηξε, τὸ δὲ βραχὺ φανίον ὤφθη
    πῦρ ψυχῆς τῇ 'μῇ καιόμενον κραδίᾳ.

69

Νὺξ ἱερὴ καὶ λύχνε, συνίστορας οὔτινας ἄλλους
    ὅρκοις ἀλλ' ὑμέας εἱλόμεθ' ἀμφότεροι·
χὠ μὲν ἐμὲ στέρξειν, κεῖνον δ' ἐγὼ οὔποτε λείψειν
    ὠμόσαμεν· κοινὴν δ' εἴχετε μαρτυρίην.
5 νῦν δ' ὁ μὲν ὅρκιά φησιν ἐν ὕδατι κεῖνα φέρεσθαι,
    λύχνε, σὺ δ' ἐν κόλποις αὐτὸν ὁρᾷς ἑτέρων.

70

Οἶδ' ὅτι μοι κενὸς ὅρκος, ἐπεὶ σέ γε τὴν φιλάσωτον
    μηνύει μυρόπνους ἀρτιβρεχὴς πλόκαμος,
μηνύει δ' ἄγρυπνον, ἰδού, βεβαρημένον ὄμμα
    καὶ σφιγκτὸς στεφάνων ἀμφὶ κόμαισι μίτος·
5 ἔσκυλται δ' ἀκόλαστα πεφυρμένος ἄρτι κίκιννος,
    πάντα δ' ὑπ' ἀκρήτου γυῖα σαλευτὰ φορεῖς.
ἔρρε, γύναι πάγκοινε, καλεῖ σε γὰρ ἡ φιλόκωμος
    πηκτὶς καὶ κροτάλων χειροτυπὴς πάταγος.

71

Ἄγγειλον τάδε, Δορκάς· ἰδοὺ πάλι δεύτερον αὐτῇ
    καὶ τρίτον ἄγγειλον, Δορκάς, ἅπαντα· τρέχε·
μηκέτι μέλλε· πέτου· βραχύ μοι βραχύ, Δορκάς, ἐπίσχες·
    Δορκάς, ποῖ σπεύδεις πρίν σε τὰ πάντα μαθεῖν;
5 πρόσθες δ' οἷς εἴρηκα πάλαι—μᾶλλον δέ—τί ληρῶ;
    μηδὲν ὅλως εἴπῃς· ἀλλ' ὅτι—πάντα λέγε·
μὴ φείδου †τὰ πάντα λέγε†· καίτοι τί σε, Δορκάς,
    ἐκπέμπω, σύν σοι καὐτὸς ἰδοὺ προάγων;

72

Ἔγνων· οὔ μ' ἔλαθες· τί θεούς; οὐ γάρ με λέληθας·
    ἔγνων· μηκέτι νῦν ὄμνυε· πάντ' ἔμαθον·
ταῦτ' ἦν, ταῦτ', ἐπίορκε· μόνη σὺ μόνη πάλιν ὑπνοῖς;
    ὦ τόλμης· καὶ νῦν νῦν ἔτι φησί, 'μόνη'.
5 οὐχ ὁ περίβλεπτός σε Κλέων; κἂν μή—τί δ' ἀπειλῶ;
    ἔρρε, κακὸν κοίτης θηρίον, ἔρρε τάχος.
καίτοι σοι δώσω τερπνὴν χάριν· οἶδ' ὅτι βούλει
    κεῖνον ὁρᾶν· αὐτοῦ δέσμιος ὧδε μένε.

73

Ἄστρα καὶ ἡ φιλέρωσι καλὸν φαίνουσα Σελήνη
    καὶ Νὺξ καὶ κώμων σύμπλανον ὀργάνιον,
ἆρά γε τὴν φιλάσωτον ἔτ' ἐν κοίταισιν ἀθρήσω
    ἄγρυπνον λύχνῳ πόλλ' †ἀποδαομένην†·
5 ἤ τιν' ἔχει σύγκοιτον; ἐπὶ προθύροισι μαράνθας
    δάκρυσιν ἐκδήσω τοὺς ἱκέτας στεφάνους
ἓν τόδ' ἐπιγράψας, 'Κύπρι, σοὶ Μελέαγρος ὁ μύστης
    σῶν κώμων στοργᾶς σκῦλα τάδ' ἐκρέμασε'.

Meleager

74

Τρισσαὶ μὲν Χάριτες, τρεῖς δὲ γλυκυπάρθενοι Ὧραι,
    τρεῖς δ᾽ ἐμὲ θηλυμανεῖς οἰστοβολοῦσι Πόθοι·
ἦ γάρ †τοι τρία τόξα κατήρισεν† ὡς ἄρα μέλλων
    οὐχὶ μίαν τρώσειν, τρεῖς δ᾽ ἐν ἐμοὶ κραδίας.

75

Ἠοῦς ἄγγελε χαῖρε Φαεσφόρε, καὶ ταχὺς ἔλθοις
    Ἕσπερος, ἣν ἀπάγεις λάθριος αὖθις ἄγων.

76

Στέρνοις μὲν Διόδωρος, ἐν ὄμμασι δ᾽ Ἡράκλειτος,
    ἡδυεπὴς δὲ Δίων, ὀσφύϊ δ᾽ Οὐλιάδης·
ἀλλὰ σὺ μὲν ψαύοις ἁπαλόχροος, ᾧ δέ, Φιλόκλεις,
    ἔμβλεπε, τῷ δὲ λάλει, τὸν δὲ τὸ λειπόμενον·
5 ὡς γνῷς οἷος ἐμὸς νόος ἄφθονος· ἢν δὲ Μυΐσκῳ
    λίχνος ἐπιβλέψῃς, μηκέτ᾽ ἴδοις τὸ καλόν.

77

Εἴ σε Πόθοι στέργουσι, Φιλοκλέες, ἥ τε μυρόπνους
    Πειθὼ καὶ κάλλευς ἀνθολόγοι Χάριτες,
ἀγκὰς ἔχοις Διόδωρον, ὁ δὲ γλυκὺς ἀντίος ᾄδοι
    Δωρόθεος, κείσθω δ᾽ εἰς γόνυ Καλλικράτης,
5 ἰαίνοι δὲ Δίων τόδ᾽ εὔστοχον ἐν χερὶ τείνων
    σὸν κέρας, Οὐλιάδης δ᾽ αὐτὸ περισκυθίσαι,
δοίη δ᾽ ἡδὺ φίλημα Φίλων, Θήρων δὲ λαλῆσαι,
    θλίβοις δ᾽ Εὐδήμου τιτθὸν ὑπὸ χλαμύδι·
εἰ γάρ σοι τάδε τερπνὰ πόροι θεός, ὦ μάκαρ, οἵαν
10   ἀρτύσεις παίδων Ῥωμαϊκὴν λοπάδα.

32

78

Πάγκαρπόν σοι Κύπρι καθήρμοσε χειρὶ τρυγήσας
    παίδων ἄνθος Ἔρως ψυχαπάτην στέφανον.
ἐν μὲν γὰρ κρίνον ἡδὺ κατέπλεξεν Διόδωρον,
    ἐν δ' Ἀσκληπιάδην τὸ γλυκὺ λευκόιον.
5 ναὶ μὴν Ἡράκλειτον ἐνέπλεκεν ὡς ἀπ' ἀκάνθης
    θεὶς ῥόδον, οἰνάνθη δ' ὥς τις ἔθαλλε Δίων.
χρυσανθῆ δὲ κόμαισι κρόκον Θήρωνα συνῆψεν,
    ἐν δ' ἔβαλ' ἑρπύλλου κλωνίον Οὐλιάδην.
ἁβροκόμην δὲ Μυΐσκον ἀειθαλὲς ἔρνος ἐλαίης,
10   ἱμερτοὺς ἀρετῆς κλῶνας, ἀπεδρέπετο.
ὀλβίστη νήσων ἱερὰ Τύρος, ἢ τὸ μυρόπνουν
    ἄλσος ἔχει παίδων Κύπριδος ἀνθοφόρων.

79

Εἰνόδιον στείχοντα μεσημβρινὸν εἶδον Ἄλεξιν
    ἄρτι κόμαν καρπῶν κειρομένου θέρεος·
διπλαῖ δ' ἀκτῖνές με κατέφλεγον, αἱ μὲν Ἔρωτος
    παιδὸς ἀπ' ὀφθαλμῶν, αἱ δὲ παρ' ἠελίου.
5 ἀλλ' ἃς μὲν νὺξ αὖθις ἐκοίμισεν, ἃς δ' ἐν ὀνείροις
    εἴδωλον μορφῆς μᾶλλον ἀνεφλόγισεν·
λυσίπονος δ' ἑτέροις ἐπ' ἐμοὶ πόνον ὕπνος ἔτευξεν
    ἔμπνουν πῦρ ψυχῇ κάλλος ἀπεικονίσας.

80

Ἡδὺ μὲν ἀκρήτῳ κεράσαι γλυκὺ νᾶμα μελισσῶν,
    ἡδὺ δὲ παιδοφιλεῖν καὐτὸν ἐόντα καλόν·
οἷα τὸν ἁβροκόμην στέργει Κλεόβουλον Ἄλεξις·
    †θνατὸν ὄντως τὸ† Κύπριδος οἰνόμελι.

81

Οὔριος ἐμπνεύσας ναύταις Νότος, ὦ δυσέρωτες,
    ἥμισύ μευ ψυχᾶς ἅρπασεν Ἀνδράγαθον.
τρὶς μάκαρες νᾶες, τρὶς δ' ὄλβια κύματα πόντου,
    τετράκι δ' εὐδαίμων παιδοφορῶν ἄνεμος·
5 εἴθ' εἴην δελφίς, ἵν' ἐμοῖς βαστακτὸς ἐπ' ὤμοις
    πορθμευθεὶς ἐσίδη τὰν γλυκύπαιδα Ῥόδον.

82

Ἀρνεῖται τὸν Ἔρωτα τεκεῖν ἡ Κύπρις ἰδοῦσα
    ἄλλον ἐν ἠιθέοις Ἵμερον Ἀντίοχον.
ἀλλά, νέοι, στέργοιτε νέον Πόθον· ἦ γὰρ ὁ κοῦρος
    εὕρηται κρείσσων οὗτος Ἔρωτος Ἔρως.

83

Εἰ χλαμύδ' εἶχεν Ἔρως καὶ μὴ πτερὰ μηδ' ἐπὶ νώτων
    τόξα τε καὶ φαρέτραν ἀλλ' ἐφόρει πέτασον,
ναὶ <μὰ> τὸν ἁβρὸν ἔφηβον ἐπόμνυμαι, Ἀντίοχος μέν
    ἦν ἂν Ἔρως, ὁ δ' Ἔρως τἄμπαλιν Ἀντίοχος.

84

Διψῶν ὡς ἐφίλησα θέρευς ἁπαλόχροα παῖδα
    εἶπα τότ' αὐχμηρὰν δίψαν ἀποπροφυγών,
Ζεῦ πάτερ, ἆρα φίλημα τὸ νεκτάρεον Γανυμήδευς
    πίνεις, καὶ τόδε σοι χείλεσιν οἰνοχοεῖ;
5 καὶ γὰρ ἐγὼ τὸν καλὸν ἐν ἠιθέοισι φιλήσας
    Ἀντίοχον ψυχῆς ἡδὺ πέπωκα μέλι'.

85

᾽Ω Χάριτες, τὸν καλὸν ᾽Αρισταγόρην ἐσιδοῦσαι
  ἀντίον εἰς τρυφερὰς ἠγκαλίσασθε χέρας·
οὕνεκα καὶ μορφᾷ βάλλει φλόγα καὶ γλυκυμυθεῖ
  καίρια καὶ σιγῶν ὄμμασι τερπνὰ λαλεῖ.
5 τηλόθι μοι πλάζοιτο· τί δὲ πλέον; ὡς παρ᾽ Ὀλύμπου
  Ζεὺς νέος οἶδεν ὁ παῖς μακρὰ κεραυνοβολεῖν.

86

Ψυχαπάται δυσέρωτες, ὅσοι φλόγα τὴν φιλόπαιδα
  οἴδατε τοῦ πικροῦ γευσάμενοι μέλιτος,
ψυχρὸν ὕδωρ νίψαι, ψυχρὸν τάχος ἄρτι τακείσης
  ἐκ χιόνος τῇ ᾽μῇ χεῖτε περὶ κραδίῃ.
5 ἦ γὰρ ἰδεῖν ἔτλην Διονύσιον· ἀλλ᾽, ὁμόδουλοι,
  πρὶν ψαῦσαι σπλάγχνων πῦρ ἀπ᾽ ἐμεῦ σβέσατε.

87

᾽Ηρκταί μευ κραδίας ψαύειν πόνος· ἦ γὰρ ἀλύων
  ἀκρονυχεὶ ταύταν ἔκνισ᾽ ὁ θερμὸς Ἔρως,
εἶπε δὲ μειδήσας, ᾽ἕξεις πάλι τὸ γλυκὺ τραῦμα,
  ὦ δύσερως, λάβρῳ καιόμενος μέλιτι᾽.
5 ἐξ οὗ δὴ νέον ἔρνος ἐν ἠιθέοις Διόφαντον
  λεύσσων οὔτε φυγεῖν οὔτε μένειν δύναμαι.

88

Αἰπολικαὶ σύριγγες ἐν οὔρεσι μηκέτι Δάφνιν
  φωνεῖτ᾽ αἰγιβάτη Πανὶ χαριζόμεναι,
μηδὲ σὺ τὸν στερχθέντα, λύρη Φοίβοιο προφῆτι,
  δάφνη παρθενίη μέλφ᾽ Ὑάκινθον ἔτι·
5 ἦν γὰρ ὅτ᾽ ἦν Δάφνις μὲν ἐν οὔρεσι, σοὶ δ᾽ Ὑάκινθος
  τερπνός· νῦν δὲ Πόθων σκῆπτρα Δίων ἐχέτω.

89

Εἰ μὴ τόξον Ἔρως μηδὲ πτερὰ μηδὲ φαρέτραν
    μηδὲ πυριβλήτους εἶχε Πόθων ἀκίδας,
οὔκ, αὐτὸν τὸν πτανὸν ἐπόμνυμαι, οὔποτ' ἂν ἔγνως
    ἐκ μορφᾶς τίς ἔφυ Ζωίλος ἢ τίς Ἔρως.

90

Ἦν καλὸς Ἡράκλειτος ὅτ' ἦν ποτε· νῦν δὲ παρ' ἥβην
    κηρύσσει πόλεμον δέρρις ὀπισθοβάταις.
ἀλλά, Πολυξενίδη, τάδ' ὁρῶν μὴ γαῦρα φρυάσσου·
    ἔστι καὶ ἐν γλουτοῖς φυομένη Νέμεσις.

91

Σιγῶν Ἡράκλειτος ἐν ὄμμασι τοῦτ' ἔπος αὐδᾷ·
    'καὶ Ζηνὸς φλέξω πῦρ τὸ κεραυνοβόλον'.
ναὶ μὴν καὶ Διόδωρος ἐνὶ στέρνοις τόδε φωνεῖ·
    'καὶ πέτρον τήκω χρωτὶ χλιαινόμενον'.
5   δύστανος, παίδων ὃς ἐδέξατο τοῦ μὲν ἀπ' ὄσσων
    λαμπάδα, τοῦ δὲ Πόθοις τυφόμενον γλυκὺ πῦρ.

92

Ἤδη μὲν γλυκὺς ὄρθρος· ὁ δ' ἐν προθύροισιν ἄυπνος
    Δᾶμις ἀποψύχει πνεῦμα τὸ λειφθὲν ἔτι
σχέτλιος Ἡράκλειτον ἰδών· ἔστη γὰρ ὑπ' αὐγάς
    ὀφθαλμῶν, βληθεὶς κηρὸς ἐς ἀνθρακιήν.
5   ἀλλά μοι ἔγρεο, Δᾶμι δυσάμμορε· καὐτὸς Ἔρωτος
    ἕλκος ἔχων ἐπὶ σοῖς δάκρυσι δακρυχέω.

93

Σοί με Πόθων δέσποινα θεὴ πόρε, σοί με, Θεόκλεις,
    ἁβροπέδιλος Ἔρως γυμνὸν ὑπεστόρεσεν
ξεῖνον ἐπὶ ξείνης δαμάσας ἀλύτοισι χαλινοῖς·
    ἱμείρω δὲ τυχεῖν ἀκλινέος φιλίης·
5 ἀλλὰ σὺ τὸν στέργοντ᾽ ἀπαναίνεαι, οὐδέ σε θέλγει
    οὐ χρόνος οὐ ξυνῆς σύμβολα σωφροσύνης.
ἵλαθ᾽, ἄναξ, ἵληθι, σὲ γὰρ θεὸν ὥρισε δαίμων·
    ἐν σοί μοι ζωῆς πείρατα καὶ θανάτου.

94

Οὐκέτι μοι Θήρων γράφεται καλός, οὐδ᾽ ὁ πυραυγής
    πρίν ποτε, νῦν δ᾽ ἤδη δαλὸς Ἀπολλόδοτος.
στέργω θῆλυν ἔρωτα· δασυτρώγλων δὲ πίεσμα
    λασταύρων μελέτω ποιμέσιν αἰγοβάταις.

95

Ἢν ἐσίδω Θήρωνα, τὰ πάνθ᾽ ὁρῶ· ἢν δὲ τὰ πάντα
    βλέψω, τόνδε δὲ μή, τἄμπαλιν οὐδὲν ὁρῶ.

96

Ἐφθέγξω, ναὶ Κύπριν, ἃ μὴ θεός, ὦ μέγα τολμᾶν
    θυμὲ μαθών· Θήρων σοὶ καλὸς οὐκ ἐφάνη·
σοὶ καλὸς οὐκ ἐφάνη Θήρων; ἀλλ᾽ αὐτὸς ὑπέστης
    οὐδὲ Διὸς πτήξας πῦρ τὸ κεραυνοβόλον;
5 τοιγάρ, ἰδού, τὸν πρόσθε λάλον προύθηκεν ἰδέσθαι
    δεῖγμα θρασυστομίης ἡ βαρύφρων Νέμεσις.

97

Ἢν τι πάθω, Κλεόβουλε,—τὸ γὰρ πλέον ἐν πυρὶ παίδων
    βαλλόμενος κεῖμαι,—λείψανον ἐν σποδιῇ,
λίσσομαι, ἀκρήτῳ μέθυσον πρὶν ὑπὸ χθόνα θέσθαι,
    κάλπιν ἐπιγράψας, 'δῶρον Ἔρως Ἀίδῃ'.

98

Λευκανθὴς Κλεόβουλος, ὁ δ᾽ ἀντία τοῦδε μελίχρους
    Σώπολις, οἱ δισσοὶ Κύπριδος ἀνθοφόροι.
τοὔνεκά μοι παίδων ἕπεται πόθος, οἱ γὰρ Ἔρωτες
    πλέξαι κἀκ λευκοῦ φασί με καὶ μέλανος.

99

Ἠγρεύθην <ὁ> πρόσθεν ἐγώ ποτε τοῖς δυσέρωσι
    κώμοις ἠιθέων πολλάκις ἐγγελάσας·
καί μ᾽ ἐπὶ σοῖς ὁ πτανὸς Ἔρως προθύροισι, Μυΐσκε,
    στῆσεν ἐπιγράψας, 'σκῦλ᾽ ἀπὸ Σωφροσύνης'.

100

Ἁβρούς, ναὶ τὸν Ἔρωτα, τρέφει Τύρος· ἀλλὰ Μυΐσκος
    ἔσβεσεν ἐκλάμψας ἀστέρας ἠέλιος.

101

Εἰ Ζεὺς κεῖνος ἔτ᾽ ἐστίν, ὁ καὶ Γανυμήδεος ἀκμὴν
    ἁρπάξας ἵν᾽ ἔχῃ νέκταρος οἰνοχόον,
πῆ μοι τὸν καλὸν ἔστιν ἐνὶ σπλάγχνοισι Μυΐσκον
    κρύπτειν, μή με λάθῃ παιδὶ βαλὼν πτέρυγας;

102

Στήσομ᾽ ἐγὼ καὶ Ζηνὸς ἐναντίον, εἴ σε, Μυΐσκε,
    ἁρπάζειν ἐθέλοι νέκταρος οἰνοχόον.
καίτοι πολλάκις αὐτὸς ἐμοὶ τάδ᾽ ἔλεξε· 'τί ταρβεῖς;
    οὔ σε βαλῶ ζήλοις· οἶδα παθὼν ἐλεεῖν'.
5 χὠ μὲν δὴ τάδε φησίν· ἐγὼ δ᾽, ἢν μυῖα παραπτῇ,
    ταρβῶ μὴ ψεύστης Ζεὺς ἐπ᾽ ἐμοὶ γέγονεν.

103

Τόν με Πόθοις ἄτρωτον ὑπὸ στέρνοισι Μυΐσκος
  ὄμμασι τοξεύσας τοῦτ᾽ ἐβόησεν ἔπος·
'τὸν θρασὺν εἷλον ἐγώ· τὸ δ᾽ ἐπ᾽ ὀφρύσι κεῖνο φρύαγμα
  σκηπτροφόρου σοφίας ἠνίδε ποσσὶ πατῶ'.
5 τῷ δ᾽ ὅσον ἀμπνεύσας τόδ᾽ ἔφην· 'φίλε κοῦρε, τί θαμβεῖς;
  καὐτὸν ἀπ᾽ Οὐλύμπου Ζῆνα καθεῖλεν Ἔρως'.

104

Ἓν καλὸν οἶδα τὸ πᾶν, ἕν μοι μόνον οἶδε τὸ λίχνον
  ὄμμα, Μυΐσκον ὁρᾶν· τἄλλα δὲ τυφλὸς ἐγώ.
πάντα δ᾽ ἐκεῖνον ἐμοὶ φαντάζεται· ἆρ᾽ ἐσορῶσιν
  ὀφθαλμοὶ ψυχῇ πρὸς χάριν οἱ κόλακες;

105

Ἤστραψε γλυκὺ κάλλος· ἰδοὺ φλόγας ὄμμασι βάλλει·
  ἆρα κεραυνομάχαν παῖδ᾽ ἀνέδειξεν Ἔρως;
χαῖρε Πόθων ἀκτῖνα φέρων θνατοῖσι, Μυΐσκε,
  καὶ λάμποις ἐπὶ γᾷ πυρσὸς ἐμοὶ φίλιος.

106

Τί κλαίεις, φρενοληστά; τί δ᾽ ἄγρια τόξα καὶ ἰούς
  ἔρριψας διφυῆ ταρσὸν ἀνεὶς πτερύγων;
ἦ ῥά γε καὶ σὲ Μυΐσκος ὁ δύσμαχος ὄμμασιν αἴθει;
  ὡς μόλις οἷ᾽ ἕδρας πρόσθε παθὼν ἔμαθες.

107

Ἡδὺς ὁ παῖς, καὶ τοὔνομ᾽ ἐμοὶ γλυκύς ἐστι Μυΐσκος
  καὶ χαρίεις· τίν᾽ ἔχω μὴ οὐχὶ φιλεῖν πρόφασιν;
καλὸς γάρ, ναὶ Κύπριν, ὅλος καλός· εἰ δ᾽ ἀνιηρός,
  οἶδε τὸ πικρὸν Ἔρως συγκεράσαι μέλιτι.

108

Ἐν σοὶ τἀμά, Μυΐσκε, βίου πρυμνήσι' ἀνῆπται,
       ἐν σοὶ καὶ ψυχῆς πνεῦμα τὸ λειφθὲν ἔτι.
ναὶ γὰρ δὴ τὰ σά, κοῦρε, τὰ καὶ κωφοῖσι λαλεῦντα
       ὄμματα, ναὶ μὰ τὸ σὸν φαιδρὸν ἐπισκύνιον,
5   ἤν μοι συννεφὲς ὄμμα βάλῃς ποτὲ χεῖμα δέδορκα,
       ἢν δ' ἱλαρὸν βλέψῃς ἡδὺ τέθηλεν ἔαρ.

109

Χειμέριον μὲν πνεῦμα, φέρει δ' ἐπὶ σοί με, Μυΐσκε,
       ἅρπαστὸν κώμοις ὁ γλυκύδακρυς Ἔρως·
χειμαίνει δὲ βαρὺς πνεύσας Πόθος· ἀλλά μ' ἐς ὅρμον
       δέξαι τὸν ναύτην Κύπριδος ἐν πελάγει.

110

Εἰκόνα μὲν Παρίην ζωογλύφος ἄνυσ' Ἔρωτος
       Πραξιτέλης Κύπριδος παῖδα τυπωσάμενος·
νῦν δ' ὁ θεῶν κάλλιστος Ἔρως ἔμψυχον ἄγαλμα
       αὑτὸν ἀπεικονίσας ἔπλασε Πραξιτέλην,
5   ὄφρ' ὁ μὲν ἐν θνατοῖς ὁ δ' ἐν αἰθέρι φίλτρα βραβεύῃ,
       γῆς θ' ἅμα καὶ μακάρων σκηπτροφορῶσι Πόθων.
ὀλβίστη Μερόπων ἱερὰ πόλις ἃ θεόπαιδα
       καινὸν Ἔρωτα νέων θρέψεν ὑφαγεμόνα.

111

Πραξιτέλης ὁ πάλαι ζωογλύφος ἁβρὸν ἄγαλμα
       ἄψυχον μορφῆς κωφὸν ἔτευξε τύπον,
πέτρον ἐνειδοφορῶν· ὁ δὲ νῦν ἔμψυχα μαγεύων
       τὸν τριπανοῦργον Ἔρωτ' ἔπλασεν ἐν κραδίᾳ.
5   ἦ τάχα τοὔνομ' ἔχει ταὐτὸν μόνον, ἔργα δὲ κρέσσων,
       οὐ λίθον ἀλλὰ φρενῶν πνεῦμα μεταρρυθμίσας.
ἵλαος πλάσσοι τὸν ἐμὸν τρόπον, ὄφρα τυπώσας
       ἐντὸς ἐμὴν ψυχὴν ναὸν Ἔρωτος ἔχῃ.

112

Οὐκ ἐθέλω Χαρίδαμον· ὁ γὰρ καλὸς εἰς Δία λεύσσει
  ὡς ἤδη τῷ θεῷ νέκταρ <ἐν>οινοχοῶν.
οὐκ ἐθέλω· τί δέ μοι τὸν ἐπουρανίων βασιλῆα
  ἄνταθλον νίκης τῆς ἐν ἔρωτι λαβεῖν;
5 ἀρκοῦμαι δ' ἢν μοῦνον ὁ παῖς ἀνιὼν ἐς Ὄλυμπον
  ἐκ γῆς νίπτρα ποδῶν δάκρυα τἀμὰ λάβῃ,
μνημόσυνον στοργῆς· γλυκὺ δ' ὄμμασι νεῦμα δίυγρον
  δοίη καί τι φίλημ' ἁρπάσαι ἀκροθιγές.
τἄλλα δὲ πάντ' ἐχέτω Ζεὺς ὡς θέμις· εἰ δ' ἐθελήσει,
10   ἢ τάχα που κἠγὼ γεύσομαι ἀμβροσίας.

113

Ζωροπότει, δύσερως, καί σου φλόγα τὰν φιλόπαιδα
  κοιμάσει λάθας δωροδότας Βρόμιος.
ζωροπότει, καὶ πλῆρες ἀφυσσάμενος σκύφος οἴνας
  ἔκκρουσον στυγερὰν ἐκ κραδίας ὀδύναν.

114

Ὤνθρωποι, βωθεῖτε· τὸν ἐκ πελάγευς ἐπὶ γαῖαν
  ἄρτι με πρωταπόπλουν ἴχνος ἐρειδόμενον
ἕλκει τῇδ' ὁ βίαιος Ἔρως· φλόγα δ' οἷα προφαίνων
  παιδὸς ἀπαστράπτει κάλλος ἐραστὸν ἰδεῖν.
5 βαίνω δ' ἴχνος ἐπ' ἴχνος, ἐν ἀέρι δ' ἡδὺ τυπωθέν
  εἶδος ἀφαρπάζων χείλεσιν ἡδὺ φιλῶ.
ἆρά γε τὴν πικρὰν προφυγὼν ἅλα πουλύ τι κείνης
  πικρότερον χέρσῳ κῦμα περῶ Κύπριδος;

115

Οἰνοπόται, δέξασθε τὸν ἐκ πελάγευς ἅμα πόντον
      καὶ κλῶπας προφυγόντ᾽ ἐν χθονὶ δ᾽ ὀλλύμενον.
ἄρτι γὰρ ἐκ νηός με μόνον πόδα θέντ᾽ ἐπὶ γαῖαν
      ἀγρεύσας ἕλκει τῆδ᾽ ὁ βίαιος Ἔρως
5   ἐνθάδ᾽ ὅπου τὸν παῖδα διαστείχοντ᾽ ἐνόησα,
      αὐτομάτοις δ᾽ ἄκων ποσσὶ ταχὺς φέρομαι.
κωμάζω δ᾽ οὐκ οἶνον ὑπὸ φρένα πῦρ δὲ γεμισθείς·
      ἀλλὰ φίλῳ, ξεῖνοι, βαιὸν ἐπαρκέσατε,
ἀρκέσατ᾽, ὦ ξεῖνοι, κἀμὲ ξενίου πρὸς Ἔρωτος
10   δέξασθ᾽ ὀλλύμενον τὸν φιλίας ἱκέτην.

116

Ὦ προδόται ψυχῆς, παίδων κύνες, αἰὲν ‹ἐν› ἰξῷ
      Κύπριδος ὀφθαλμοὶ βλέμματα χριόμενοι,
ἡρπάσατ᾽ ἄλλον ἔρωτ᾽, ἄρνες λύκον, οἷα κορώνη
      σκορπίον, ὡς τέφρη πῦρ ὑποθαλπόμενον.
5   δρᾶθ᾽ ὅ τι καὶ βούλεσθε· τί μοι νενοτισμένα χεῖτε
      δάκρυα, πρὸς δ᾽ ἱκέτην αὐτομολεῖτε τάχος;
ὀπτᾶσθ᾽ ἐν κάλλει, τύφεσθ᾽ ὑποκαόμενοι νῦν,
      ἄκρος ἐπεὶ ψυχῆς ἐστι μάγειρος Ἔρως.

117

Ἡδύ τί μοι διὰ νυκτὸς ἐνύπνιον ἁβρὰ γελῶντος
      ὀκτωκαιδεκέτους παιδὸς ἔτ᾽ ἐν χλαμύδι
ἤγαγ᾽ Ἔρως ὑπὸ χλαῖναν· ἐγὼ δ᾽ ἁπαλῷ περὶ χρωτί
      στέρνα βαλὼν κενεὰς ἐλπίδας ἐδρεπόμην.
5   καί μ᾽ ἔτι νῦν θάλπει μνήμης πόθος, ὄμμασι δ᾽ ὕπνον
      ἀγρευτὴν πτηνοῦ φάσματος αἰὲν ἔχω.
ὦ δύσερως ψυχή, παῦσαί ποτε καὶ δι᾽ ὀνείρων
      εἰδώλοις κάλλευς κωφὰ χλιαινομένη.

118

Ὀρθροβόας δυσέρωτι κακάγγελε, νῦν, τρισάλαστε,
    ἐννύχιος κράζεις πλευροτυπῆ κέλαδον
γαῦρος ὑπὲρ κοίτας, ὅτε μοι βραχὺ τοῦτ' ἔτι νυκτός
    παιδοφιλεῖν, ἐπ' ἐμαῖς δ' ἁδὺ γελᾷς ὀδύναις;
5 ἆδε φίλα θρεπτῆρι χάρις; ναὶ τὸν βαθὺν ὄρθρον,
    ἔσχατα γηρύσει ταῦτα τὰ πικρὰ μέλη.

119

Κύπρις ἐμοὶ ναύκληρος, Ἔρως δ' οἴακα φυλάσσει
    ἄκρον ἔχων ψυχῆς ἐν χερὶ πηδάλιον·
χειμαίνει δ' ὁ βαρὺς πνεύσας Πόθος, οὔνεκα δὴ νῦν
    παμφύλῳ παίδων νήχομαι ἐν πελάγει.

120

Τίς τάδε μοι θνητῶν <τὰ> περὶ θριγκοῖσιν ἀνῆψεν
    σκῦλα, παναισχίστην τέρψιν Ἐνυαλίου;
οὔτε γὰρ αἰγανέαι περιαγέες οὔτε τι πῆληξ
    ἄλλοφος οὔτε φόνῳ χρανθὲν ἄρηρε σάκος,
5 ἀλλ' αὔτως γανόωντα καὶ ἀστυφέλικτα σιδάρῳ
    οἷά περ οὐκ ἐνοπᾶς ἀλλὰ χορῶν ἔναρα·
οἷς θάλαμον κοσμεῖτε γαμήλιον· ὅπλα δὲ λύθρῳ
    λειβόμενα βροτέῳ σηκὸς Ἄρηος ἔχοι.

121

—Ὤνθρωφ', Ἡράκλειτος ἐγὼ σοφὰ μοῦνος ἀνευρών.
    —φαμί, τὰ δ' ἐς πάτραν—κρέσσονα καὶ σοφίας·
λὰξ γὰρ καὶ τοκεῶνας.—Ἰὼ ξένε, δύσφρονας ἄνδρας
    ὑλάκτευν.—Λαμπρὰ θρεψαμένοισι χάρις.
5 —Οὐκ ἀπ' ἐμεῦ;—Μὴ τρηχύς, ἐπεὶ τάχα καὶ σύ τι πεύσῃ
    τρηχύτερον πάτρας.—Χαῖρε.—Σὺ δ' ἐξ Ἐφέσου.

122

Ἀ στάλα, σύνθημα τί σοι γοργωπὸς ἀλέκτωρ
    ἔστα καλλαΐνᾳ σκαπτροφόρος πτέρυγι
ποσσὶν ὑφαρπάζων νίκας κλάδον, ἄκρα δ' ἐπ' αὐτᾶς
    βαθμῖδος προπεσὼν κέκλιται ἀστράγαλος;
5 ἦ ῥά γε νικάεντα μάχᾳ σκαπτοῦχον ἄνακτα
    κρύπτεις; ἀλλὰ τί σοι παίγνιον ἀστράγαλος;
πρὸς δ' ἔτι λιτὸς ὁ τύμβος· ἐπιπρέπει ἀνδρὶ πενιχρῷ
    ὄρνιθος κλαγγαῖς νυκτὸς ἀνεγρομένῳ.
οὐ δοκέω, σκάπτρον γὰρ ἀναίνεται· ἀλλὰ σὺ κεύθεις
10   ἀθλοφόρον νίκαν ποσσὶν ἀειράμενον;
οὐ ψαύω καὶ τᾷδε· τί γὰρ ταχὺς εἴκελος ἀνήρ
    ἀστραγάλῳ; νῦν δὴ τὠτρεκὲς ἐφρασάμαν·
φοῖνιξ οὐ νίκαν ἐνέπει, πάτραν δὲ μεγαυχῆ
    ματέρα Φοινίκων τὰν πολύπαιδα Τύρον·
15 ὄρνις δ' ὅττι γεγωνὸς ἀνὴρ καί που περὶ Κύπριν
    πρᾶτος κἠν Μούσαις ποικίλος ὑμνοθέτας·
σκᾶπτρα δ' ἔχει σύνθημα λόγου, θνάσκειν δὲ πεσόντα
    οἰνοβρεχῆ προπετὴς ἐννέπει ἀστράγαλος.
καὶ δὴ σύμβολα ταῦτα· τὸ δ' οὔνομα πέτρος ἀείδει,
20   Ἀντίπατρον προγόνων φύντ' ἀπ' ἐρισθενέων.

123

Οὐ γάμον ἀλλ' Ἀίδαν ἐπινυμφίδιον Κλεαρίστα
    δέξατο παρθενίας ἄμματα λυομένα.
ἄρτι γὰρ ἑσπέριοι νύμφας ἐπὶ δικλίσιν ἄχευν
    λωτοί, καὶ θαλάμων ἐπλαταγεῦντο θύραι.
5 ἠῷοι δ' ὀλολυγμὸν ἀνέκραγον, ἐκ δ' Ὑμέναιος
    σιγαθεὶς γοερὸν φθέγμα μεθαρμόσατο.
αἱ δ' αὐταὶ καὶ φέγγος ἐδᾳδούχουν περὶ παστῷ
    πεῦκαι καὶ φθιμένᾳ νέρθεν ἔφαινον ὁδόν.

124

Παμμῆτορ Γῆ, χαῖρε· σὺ τὸν πάρος οὐ βαρὺν εἰς σέ
Αἰσιγένην καὐτὴ νῦν ἐπέχοις ἀβαρής.

125

Οἰκτρότατον μάτηρ σε, Χαρίξενε, δῶρον ἐς Ἅιδαν
  ὀκτωκαιδεκέταν ἐστόλισ᾽ ἐν χλαμύδι·
ἦ γὰρ δὴ καὶ πέτρος ἀνέστενεν ἁνίκ᾽ ἀπ᾽ οἴκων
  ἄλικες οἰμωγᾷ σὸν νέκυν ἠχθοφόρευν.
5 πένθος δ᾽, οὐχ ὑμέναιον, ἀνωρύοντο γονῆες·
  αἰαῖ τὰς μαστῶν ψευδομένας χάριτας
καὶ κενεὰς ὠδῖνας· ἰὼ κακοπάρθενε Μοῖρα,
  στεῖρα γονᾶς στοργὰν ἔπτυσας εἰς ἀνέμους·
τοῖς μὲν ὁμιλήσασι ποθεῖν πάρα, τοῖς δὲ τοκεῦσι
10   πενθεῖν, οἷς δ᾽ ἀγνὼς πευθομένοις ἐλεεῖν.

126

Οὐκέθ᾽ ὁμοῦ χιμάροισιν ἔχειν βίον, οὐκέτι ναίειν
  ὁ τραγόπους ὀρέων Πὰν ἐθέλω κορυφάς.
τί γλυκύ μοι, τί ποθεινὸν ἐν οὔρεσιν; ὤλετο Δάφνις,
  Δάφνις ὃς ἡμετέρῃ πῦρ ἔτεκ᾽ ἐν κραδίῃ.
5 ἄστυ τόδ᾽ οἰκήσω, θηρῶν δέ τις ἄλλος ἐπ᾽ ἄγρην
  στελλέσθω· τὰ πάροιθ᾽ οὐκέτι Πανὶ φίλα.

127

Αἱ Νύμφαι τὸν Βάκχον, ὅτ᾽ ἐκ πυρὸς ἦλαθ᾽ ὁ κοῦρος,
  νίψαν ὑπὲρ τέφρης ἄρτι κυλιόμενον·
τοὔνεκα σὺν Νύμφαις Βρόμιος φίλος· ἢν δέ νιν εἴργῃς
  μίσγεσθαι, δέξῃ πῦρ ἔτι καιόμενον.

128

Τανταλὶ παῖ Νιόβα, κλύ' ἐμὰν φάτιν ἄγγελον ἄτας·
  δέξαι σῶν ἀχέων οἰκτροτάταν λαλιάν.
λῦε κόμας ἀνάδεσμον, ἰὼ βαρυπενθέσι Φοίβου
  γειναμένα τόξοις ἀρσενόπαιδα γόνον·
5 οὔ σοι παῖδες ἔτ' εἰσίν. ἀτὰρ τί τόδ' ἄλλο; τί λεύσσω;
  αἰαῖ πλημμύρει παρθενικαῖσι φόνος·
ἁ μὲν γὰρ ματρὸς περὶ γούνασιν, ἁ δ' ἐνὶ κόλποις
  κέκλιται, ἁ δ' ἐπὶ γᾶς, ἁ δ' ἐπιμαστίδιος,
ἄλλα δ' ἀντωπὸν θαμβεῖ βέλος, ἁ δ' ὑπ' ὀιστοῖς
10 πτώσσει, τᾶς δ' ἔμπνουν ὄμμ' ἔτι φῶς ὁράᾳ.
ἁ δὲ λάλον στέρξασα πάλαι στόμα, νῦν ὑπὸ θάμβευς
  μάτηρ σαρκοτακὴς οἷα πέπηγε λίθος.

129

Ἁ πύματον καμπτῆρα καταγγέλλουσα κορωνίς,
  ἑρκοῦρος γραπταῖς πιστοτάτα σελίσιν,
φαμὶ τὸν ἐκ πάντων ἠθροισμένον εἰς ἕνα μόχθον
  ὑμνοθετᾶν βύβλῳ τᾷδ' ἐνελιξάμενον
5 ἐκτελέσαι Μελέαγρον, ἀείμνηστον δὲ Διοκλεῖ
  ἄνθεσι συμπλέξαι μουσοπόλον στέφανον.
οὖλα δ' ἐγὼ καμφθεῖσα δρακοντείοις ἴσα νώτοις
  σύνθρονος ἵδρυμαι τέρμασιν εὐμαθίας.

130

—Εἶπον ἀνειρομένῳ τίς καὶ τίνος ἐσσί. Φ. Φίλαυλος
  Εὐκρατίδεω.—Ποδαπὸς δ' εὔχεαι < >
—Ἔζησας δὲ τίνα στέργων βίον; Φ. Οὐ τὸν ἀρότρου
  οὐδὲ τὸν ἐκ νηῶν, τὸν δὲ σοφοῖς ἔταρον.
5 —Γήραϊ δ' ἢ νούσῳ βίον ἔλλιπες; Φ. Ἤλυθον Ἅιδην
  αὐτοθελεὶ Κείων γευσάμενος κυλίκων.
—Ἦ πρέσβυς; Φ. Καὶ κάρτα.—Λάβοι νύ σε βῶλος ἐλαφρή
  σύμφωνον πινυτῷ σχόντα λόγῳ βίοτον.

46

131

Εἰ καί σοι πτέρυγες ταχιναὶ περὶ νῶτα τέτανται
    καὶ Σκυθικῶν τόξων ἀκροβολεῖς ἀκίδας,
φεύξομ', Ἔρως, ὑπὸ γᾶν σε· τί δὲ πλέον; οὐδὲ γὰρ αὐτός
    σὰν ἔφυγεν ῥώμαν πανδαμάτωρ Ἀίδας.

132

Δεξιτερὴν Ἀίδαο θεοῦ χέρα καὶ τὰ κελαινά
    ὄμνυμεν ἀρρήτου δέμνια Περσεφόνης,
παρθένοι ὡς ἔτυμον καὶ ὑπὸ χθονί· πολλὰ δ' ὁ πικρός
    αἰσχρὰ καθ' ἡμετέρης ἔβλυσε παρθενίης
5 Ἀρχίλοχος· ἐπέων δὲ καλὴν φάτιν οὐκ ἐπὶ καλά
    ἔργα, γυναικεῖον δ' ἔτραπεν ἐς πόλεμον.
Πιερίδες, τί κόρῃσιν ἔφ' ὑβριστῆρας ἰάμβους
    ἐτράπετ', οὐχ ὁσίῳ φωτὶ χαριζόμεναι;

COMMENTARY

1

Meleager's Garland (*A. P.* 4.1)

This, the longest of Meleager's poems, served as an introduction to
his *Stephanos*. It dedicates the entire anthology to Diocles, and then
lists all of the poets to be included in the collection, forty-seven in
all, excluding Meleager himself. Each of the poets is associated
with a flower or some other form of vegetation, confirming the ini-
tial conceit that they have all been bound together in a "garland".

Although poetry, flowers, and herbs were regularly associated
with one another in Greek poetry, this is apparently the first
attempt to associate the qualities of particular flowers with those of
particular writers. At times such parallels between plant and poet
do not appear to be appropriate.

Throughout his extant poetry Meleager demonstrates a fond-
ness for flowers. Whether this preference is intrinsic to Meleager's
poetic expression or simply a device for extending the conceit of
the *Stephanos* cannot be ascertained. Greek plant names were
never systematized, and the same names were frequently used for
more than one plant, even unrelated ones; thus many of
Meleager's flowers, shrubs, fruits, and foliage cannot be identified
with certainty, and the imprecision of poets in such details only
obfuscates the matter further.

No discoverable organizational principle links the introduction
to the remainder of the *Garland*. Poems were apparently grouped
by subject matter, subordinating lesser poets to major ones and
emphasizing the rehandling and reshaping of similar topoi.
In the introduction some poets are allotted a full line, while
others are paired in couplets, or grouped in threes for every two
couplets. The arrangement is neither chronological nor manipu-
lated to give prominence to more distinguished contributors.
Occasionally there is evidence of grouping by period or sex, but
without consistency.

Several poets cited in Meleager's introduction (Euphemus,
Melanippides, Parthenis, Polyclitus) have not survived into the
Palatine Anthology, and other poets cited (Anacreon, Archilochus,

49

Bacchylides, Melanippus, Sappho, Simonides) predate Hellenistic times, if their ascriptions are correct.

2 ὑμνοθετᾶν: A genitive plural.

3 Diocles, to whom the *Garland* is dedicated, appears only here and in Selection 129 (*A. P.* 12.257), the closing epigram of the cycle. He is ἀριζάλῳ, we must assume, because of his immortalization in the poet's verse.

4 μναμόσυνον: "keepsake".

5 Anyte's *floruit* has been established about 300 B.C. She was an able composer of epigrammatic quatrains, twenty-four of which survive, many in the form of sepulchral inscriptions. She also composed lyric poetry and hexameters. Moero was Byzantine by birth and a near contemporary of Anyte. Ten of her hexameter verses are extant, but none of her lyric poetry. We are told by Meleager that there were "many lilies of Moero", but only two of her epigrams are to be found in the *Palatine Anthology* (6.119, 189).

6 The two epigrams attributed to Sappho in the *Palatine Anthology* (7.489, 505) and the one headed ὡς Σαπφοῦς (6.269) are perhaps Hellenistic and not those of the seventh and sixth century B.C. lyric poet from Lesbos.

7 Melanippides' identity is indeterminate. He may have been a sixth- or fifth-century epicist and writer of epigrams, or his grandson, but at any rate he appears to be pre-Hellenistic. He is not included in the *Anthology* as it has been transmitted to us. His entries either were excluded by later anthologists or may still be carried in the collection with anonymous ascriptions. ἔγκυον: "bursting with".

8 The *Greek Anthology* preserves most of the more than one hundred epigrams attributed to the sixth- or fifth-century lyricist and elegist Simonides. It is impossible to identify the epigrams he may actually have written from the Hellenistic ones ascribed to him. νέον κλῆμα: "fresh cutting".

9-10 μυρόπνουν: An appealing play on the meaning of the word, "sweet-voiced" and "fragrant". Nossis is represented by twelve epigrams in the *Anthology*. Like Anyte, she wrote in quatrains and was known as a lyric poet. Of the epigrams ascribed to her in the *Anthology* only one is erotic (*A. P.* 5.170). It has been suggested that it is this one which prompted Meleager to say that "Eros melted the wax with which she covered her writing tablets."

11 σάμψυχον: "marjoram". Rhianus enjoys only a slim existence outside of the *Anthology*, which contains ten of his epigrams. His reputation in antiquity rested on his writing of historical epics such as the *Messeniaca*, the *Heracleia*, the *Achaeica*, and the *Thessalica*. He wrote during the second half of the third century B.C.

12 Although we have little of what Erinna is known to have written (she is represented by three epigrams in the *Anthology*), what remains, especially *The Distaff*, is much discussed. παρθενόχρωτα: While we are told of the existence of white crocuses which would satisfy the sense, the adjective might also apply to the texture of skin and so to that of a petal.

13 Meleager is possibly referring to Alcaeus, the seventh century lyricist, but he more probably means Alcaeus of Messene, to whom Gow and Page assign twenty-two epigrams in the *Anthology*. Alcaeus of Messene (*floruit* 215-195 B.C.) also wrote abusive iambics and a "critical" parody on the plagiarism of the historian Ephorus. λάληθρον: "prattling". Gow and Page suggest that the markings on flowers had no significance until the conceits of poets gave them a voice. See, for example, the story that from the blood of Hyacinthus sprang a flower on whose leaves appeared the exclamation AI, or the letter Υ, the initial letter of Ὑάκινθος. (See as well Ovid, *Met.* 10.161-219.)

14 Samius is a shadowy figure represented by two epigrams in the *Anthology* (6.114, 116), both concerned with Philip V of Macedon.

15 Leonidas of Tarentum (*floruit* middle of the third century B.C.) was a prolific writer of epigrams, one hundred and three of which are preserved, for the most part, in the *Anthology*. θαλεροὺς κορύμβους: "fresh and vigorous flower clusters".

16 Mnasalcas (*floruit* about 275 B.C.) is represented by seventeen epigrams in the *Anthology*. κόμας ὀξυτόρου πίτυος: "needle tips of sharp pine".

17 πλατάνιστον is apparently the offending word in this sentence, since it complements none of the other nouns or adjectives. Gow and Page suggest that πλατάνιστον conceals some word meaning "tendril-....". We know nothing of Pamphilus. The *Anthology* contains two of his epigrams.

18 Three quatrains of Pancrates survive in the *Greek Anthology*.

Meleager

He is cited by Athenaeus of Naucratis as an epicist and elegist. καρύης: "of the walnut tree".

19 Tymnes' (perhaps third century) preference for quatrains and his animal epigrams (the *Greek Anthology* contains seven of his epigrams in all) suggest that he was influenced by Anyte. σίσυμ- βρον: "water cress", but this seems inappropriate for a wreath. Gow and Page suggest *mentha aquatica*, recalling the imprecision with which Greeks named their plants.

20 Nicias (*floruit* during the first half of the third century B.C.) may be the physician friend of Theocritus (see *Idyll* 28). Eight epigrams are attributed to him in the *Anthology*. None of Euphemus' epigrams have survived. ἀμμότροφον: "growing in sand", and so "on the shore", but the plant πάραλον cannot be identified.

21 Damagetus (*floruit* during the last quarter of the third century B.C.) was apparently a member of the Peloponnesian school of epigrammatists. One of his epigrams concerns the dedication of hair made by Arsinoë, daughter of Ptolemy III, in the temple of Artemis in Alexandria, and suggests that Damagetus was connected with the Egyptian court. A dozen of Damagetus' epigrams are included in the *Anthology*.

22 Callimachus (*floruit* 305-240 B.C.), the quintessential Alexandrian, apparently enjoyed universal fame and popularity. His most famous scholarly work, the *Pinakes*, was the first scientific literary history of which we know. In addition to epigrams he wrote literary hymns, the *Aetia*, an epyllion called the *Hecale*, elegies, and lyrics. The meaning of στυφελοῦ…μέλιτος is somewhat obscure, unless it means, as Gow and Page suggest, "full of bitter 'honey-dew'", that is, the substance deposited by insects on trees.

23 λυχνίδα: "rose-campion". Euphorion (275 B.C.—end of the third century) appears to have written *epyllia* and composite epics on mythological subjects in addition to his epigrams. ἄμεινον is meaningless, and the corruption of the text is at present insoluble. It is possible that a couplet containing the name of a flower has dropped out. There have been numerous suggestions, such as κυκλάμινον and κινάμωνον, to replace ἄμεινον, but such changes obscure the meaning of ἐν Μούσῃσιν.

24 Διὸς ἐκ κούρων: This strange circumlocution stands for Dioscorides (last half of the third century B.C.). There is no evidence that he wrote anything but epigrams, of which forty are found in the *Greek Anthology*.

25 τῆσι lacks an antecedent; but if a couplet is missing, then the feminine plural could have indicated Dioscorides' flowers. Nothing is known of Hegesippus (*floruit* middle of the third century B.C.). In some of his epigrams (there are eight in the *Anthology*), he seems to have imitated Nicias and Callimachus. μαινάδα βότρυν: "intoxicating grape".

26 Perses (end of the fourth century B.C.) is one of the earliest Hellenistic epigrammatists included in the *Anthology*.   εὐώδη σχοῖνον: "ginger-grass".

27 γλυκύμηλον: "summer apple".   Three Diotimuses are represented in the *Anthology*. Ten epigrams are tentatively assigned to a Hellenistic Diotimus dating from the first half of the third century B.C.

28 Three epigrams represent Menecrates' extant contribution to the *Anthology*. His *floruit* has been tentatively set at the end of the second century B.C.

29 μυρραίους: "redolent of myrrh".   Nicaenetus is dated to the second half of the third century B.C. Five epigrams from various sources bear his name, and he is known to have written a *Catalogue of Women* which is no longer extant.   Phaennus, perhaps datable to the third century, is represented by two epigrams.

30 βλωθρήν ἀχράδα: "wild pear".   The early third-century lyricist Simias is best known for his τεχνοπαίγνια; three of these "pattern poems"—the *Axe*, the *Egg*, and the *Wings*—are in the *Anthology*.

32 βαιὰ διακνίζων: "dividing in small pieces".   No epigrams of Parthenis have survived, whose name, depending on its accentuation, may be masculine or feminine.

34 Two epigrams in the *Anthology* ascribed to the fifth-century lyric poet Bacchylides are accepted as genuine. His famous *Odes* survive, as do fragments of his σκόλια (drinking songs).

35-36 In saying that he wove in "Anacreon, that sweet song, nectar [genitive of description], a blossom, yes, but out of place among elegies", Meleager seems to apologize (as in the case of Archilochus below) for excluding extended selections of the well-known lyricist (late sixth and early fifth century).

37 φορβῆς: "fodder".   σκολιότριχος: "with curly leaves".

38 Archilochus, the master of iambic meter, flourished from

Meleager

714-676 B.C. and was one of the earliest lyric poets of Greece. The couplets ascribed to him in the *Anthology* are of doubtful authenticity.

39 Alexander of Aetolia (*floruit* at the beginning of the third century B.C.) worked in the great library at Alexandria and was responsible for its collections of tragic and satyric drama. He was a tragic poet himself and a writer of elegy and epic. Two of his epigrams survive in the *Greek Anthology*.

40 No epigrams of Polyclitus are found in the *Anthology*, and no other source refers to him.

41 ἀμάρακον: "marjoram". Polystratus' only epigram states that the Roman destruction of Corinth (146 B.C.) was a suitable reprisal for the Greek destruction of Troy (*A. P.* 12. 91).

42 κύπρον: "henna". The adjective Phoenissian is appropriate since Antipater (*floruit* during the first half of the second century B.C.) came from Sidon. Sixty-eight epigrams, mostly found in the *Greek Anthology*, are attributed to him. He was apparently also a rhetorician.

44 "The poet we sing of as the gift of Hermes", and so Hermadorus. One epigram is hesitantly assigned to him in the *Palatine Anthology*.

45 Posidippus (about 310 to 250 B.C.) wrote an *Aethiopia* and an *Asopia*. Twenty-three epigrams drawn from various sources are assigned to him. Hedylus (second half of the third century B.C.) apparently wrote prose works as well as poetry. Twelve of his epigrams are preserved in the *Greek Anthology*. ἄγρι' ἀρούρης: Gow and Page suggest that "wild flowers of the cornfield" might be poppies, since they are mentioned nowhere else in Meleager's introduction.

46 Sicelides (*floruit* 290-265 B.C.) is known in some sources as Asclepiades. It is impossible to determine his primary name. He may have written lyrics and hexameters in addition to his forty-seven epigrams in the *Anthology*. ἀνέμοις ἄνθεα φυόμενα: "anemones".

47-48 χρύσειον κλῶνα: "the golden bough" appears to be a tree or a shrub but cannot be identified. About thirty epigrams are attributed to the fourth century philosopher Plato, some apparently Hellenistic, others post-Meleagrian.

49 Aratus lived from about 315 B.C. to about 240 B.C. He is best known for his *Phaenomena*, a work still extant, in which, at the request of Antigonus Gonatas, the king of Macedonia, Aratus versified the astronomical treatises of Eudoxus of Cnidus. Two of Aratus' epigrams are in the *Anthology*. οὐρανομάκευς: "reaching to heaven", but referring to the *Phaenomena*, not to the height of the palms.

50 ἕλικας: these, apparently, are the newly sprouted leaves on the summit of the tree.

51 λωτόν: perhaps a "water-lily"; but the word is used to denote several species of plants and trees. φλογὶ: "phlox". The name Chaeremon is a common one, discouraging every attempt to establish his identity, date, or origin. The *Anthology* contains three of his epigrams.

52 Biographical evidence for Phaedimus (first half of third century B.C.) is almost non-existent. Two of his four epigrams in the *Anthology* are in meters other than elegiac, suggesting that he lived early in the third century, since poems in the *Anthology* that use experimental forms are found only during this period. Antagoras (*floruit* 270-260 B.C.) has left us two epigrams. There is mention of his *Thebais*, and we know that he was associated with other poets at the court of Antigonus Gonatas. Unless εὔστροφον describes the poet, its meaning is obscure. "Coweye" is defined in our sources as a "house-leek". Gow and Page suggest that ὄμμα βοός may be a climbing plant such as the convolvulus.

53 φιλάκρητον: The point of the adjective is not clear, since no sympotic epigram is included among the nineteen epigrams by Theodoridas (second half of the third century) in the *Anthology*.

54 ἕρπυλλον: "thyme". Phanias is no more than a name in literary chronicles. A clue in one of his eight epigrams suggests that he knew Latin as well as Greek.

55 ἄλλων...νεόγραφα: "many newly written buds of others"; that is, contemporary poetry.

56 καὶ...λευκόια: "in addition to the early snowdrops of his own", i.e., Meleager's.

57-58 Perhaps, "But although I extend this offering (the book) to my friends, this sweet-voiced garland of the Muses is the common property of initiates of the arts". ἡδυεπὴς a παρὰ προσδοκίαν for "sweet-smelling".

Meleager

2

Epitaph 1 (*A. P.* 7. 417)
This is the first of three sequential "epitaphs" found in the *Garland* which serve as biographical notes on the author's life. Each offers additional, though limited, information about Meleager. Such "autobiographies" were common among epigrammatists (see Callimachus, *A. P.* 7. 525 and 526). To these three we should add the anonymous epigram just preceding them (*A. P.* 416, to be found on page vi of this text) and a "riddle-epitaph" (Selection 5: *A. P.* 7. 421).

1-2 Gadara is called "Attic" by Meleager presumably because the city was renowned for the writers and intellectuals it had fostered. Among these were Menippus and Philodemus, who are discussed in the *Introduction*. Gadara was located at the modern-day site of Ramoth-Gilead in Syria.

3 Εὐκράτεω: genitive case. Meleager here names his father.

4 Μενιππείοις Χάρισιν: The poet refers to a prose work, the *Graces*, of which we have no trace. It is not surprising that he should be interested in Menippus and proficient in writing Menippean satire, since both writers were natives of the same city. Such satire is best exemplified in extant ancient literature by the dialogues of Lucian. One of Lucian's satires bears the name *Menippus*, and Menippus figures frequently in his *Dialogues of the Dead*. Marcus Terentius Varro's *Saturae Menippeae* are fragmentary. συντροχάσας: "to run neck and neck"; this pleasing metaphor is more forceful than a simple statement of competition, and plays lightly on the equine connotation of Menippus' name.

5-6 For these sentiments see *Introduction*, page 2.

7 ἐχάραξα: The verb means first "to make pointed" and then by extension "to scratch" and "to inscribe", suggesting Meleager's use of wax tablets.

3

Epitaph 2 (*A. P.* 7. 418)
2 ἤνδρωσεν: He was born in Gadara, but Tyre "made a man" of him.

3 Δία: accusative case. The "Zeus" in question is Cos' most famous son, Ptolemy II Philadelphus (309-247 B.C.), patron of poets and artists, and promoter of the great library and museum at

Alexandria.

4 θετὸν: "an adoptive child". **Μερόπων**: The reference to Meropes is elusive. The city of Cos was known as Cos Meropis, to distinguish it from an earlier capital of the island. It would appear that Meleager was made *proxenos*.

6 ἠγλάισαν: The adjective ἀγλαός is occasionally applied to the Muses. It is appropriate that they should endow a poet with their own quality.

4

Epitaph 3 (*A. P.* 7. 419)

2 ὕπνον ὀφειλόμενον is a cliché for "death". The phrase recalls the Homeric turn (*Il.* 11. 241) κοιμήσατο χάλκεον ὕπνον.

3-4 These two lines summarize well Meleager's style, since he did indeed "clothe sweet-teared Love and the Muses with good-humored elegance."

5 θεόπαις: Gow and Page suggest that this word (usually applied to Eros) must mean "of god-like boys", a logical interpretation in view of some of the later epigrams. **ἤνδρωσε**: See Selection 3 (*A. P.* 7. 418. 2).

7 σαλάμ: "salaam", the sole appearance of the word in extant Greek literature.

8 ναίδιος: We must assume that this is a Phoenician word, similar in meaning to σαλάμ and χαῖρε. **τὸ δ' αὐτὸ φράσον**: "and you, say the same (to me)".

5

A Riddle (*A. P.* 7. 421)

Riddle epitaphs frequently appear in Hellenistic epigram (see especially the sequence by Leonidas, Meleager, Antipater and Alcaeus [*A. P.* 7. 422-429]), but Meleager's treatment is distinctive and exemplifies the determination of Alexandrian poets to seek variety within the narrow limits of the epigrammatic tradition to which they adhered. The tomb in this case is Meleager's own; thus the epigram serves as a variation on the previous three "biographies". The figure on the tombstone as Meleager the poet is identified by rejection of the more likely meanings of the symbols ("it is not this, it is not that") until the solution becomes apparent.

1 σιβύνας: "hunting spear" (masculine singular).

Meleager

2 This type of double question is customary in Greek drama. στάλας is a genitive singular.

3-4 The suggestion that it is Eros, the most famous of winged symbols, is rejected as inappropriate to a tombstone; nor are the accoutrements appropriate to him.

4-6 Another possibility is dismissed: Chronos, although winged, is old, not young like the representation on the stele. Supply ἐνέπω from line 3. τριγέρων: the prefix τρι- is used here, as frequently in Greek, to indicate an indefinite number (cf. the English usage, "hundreds of...").

8 σὺ δ' ὁ πτερόεις...λόγος: The expression is troublesome; but, as Gow and Page suggest, it must mean, "you, the one with wings, [representing] his name, are Literature".

9-10 This couplet summarizes neatly Meleager's literary accomplishments. ἄμφηκες γέρας: "two-edged attribute [of Leto's daughter]". The spear with its double head can symbolize both the elegiac couplet which is the vehicle of Meleager's epigrams (the μέτρον ἐρωτογράφον) and perhaps the combination of seriousness and hilarity in Meleager's prose satires.

11 Now that the profession of the "deceased" has been determined, the field of possibilities is narrowed and the connection between the symbol representing Meleager the hunter and Meleager the poet becomes clear. The mythological Meleager, son of Oeneus, was renowned as the slayer of a monstrous boar which ravaged Calydon; thus the attributes of hunting spear and boar skin depicted on the stele. Meleager's victory over the animal signaled his own death, since, in the squabble over its possession, he slew his brothers. To avenge their death his mother recalled a prophecy which had been made to her at his birth by the Fates, to the effect that as soon as the log burning on the hearth was consumed, Meleager would die. In her maternal concern she had retrieved it and hidden it away in a chest. Now she brought it out and threw it on the fire. As it crackled into ashes, Meleager expired. (See Apollodor. 1. 8. 2-3 as well as Ovid, *Met.* 8. 270-545.)

13 χαῖρε καὶ ἐν φθιμένοισιν: "even though you are among the dead". Ἔρωτι: The dative here is troublesome. The genitive has been suggested as more appropriate: this whole phrase would then mean "you harnessed into one craft the Muse of Love and the *Graces* [that is, his Menippean satires]".

6

Δεινὸς Ἔρως (A. P. 5. 176)

We come now to the heart of Meleager's poetry. This short epigram is characteristic of Meleager's style at its best. The language is spare, yet poetic. The final line is felicitous and carries with it the turn associated with more modern epigrams. The images of fire and water are popular ones with Meleager. For a commentary on the dual nature of Eros, see H. Ouvré, *Méléagre de Gadara* (Paris 1894) 119 ff.

1 τί δὲ τὸ πλέον: "what is the advantage (for me)...?"

3 πυκνὰ: "often" or "constantly".

4 καὶ: "and even".

7

The Eternal Chase (A. P. 5. 179)

We have here a fine example of Meleager's ability to "develop" an epigram. Throughout the ten lines there is a constant shift in situation and mood, as the exultant and determined lover bit by bit loses confidence in his prowess. Meleager finally reverses the usual motif, whereby it is mortals who are the prey of Love, by making Love the prey of a mortal.

1 Aphrodite is called Κύπριν because of the popularity of her worship on the island of Cyprus.

3 φλέξω ναί: A good example of aposiopesis. The full phrase would perhaps have read φλέξω ναὶ ᾿Αφροδίτην. σιμὰ: "with your nose in the air".

4 σαρδάνιον: "Sardonic" is not used here in the common sense, but suggests the forced smile of someone in pain. The σαρδάνιον was a bitter-tasting plant.

5 σευ is genitive singular. ὠκύπτερα is best treated as a substantive; translate the phrase, "your swift wings, the guides to Passion".

7 A "Cadmean victory" was one won at a great price, and recalls the legend of Cadmus' sowing of dragon's teeth. From each tooth sprang an armed man, but the fighting among the warriors was so heavy that only five survived.

8 λύγκα: Not a wolf, but a lynx, a bright-eyed, watchful and crafty creature—a splendid image to represent Eros, the prisoner.

9 δυσνίκητε: "hard to conquer". ἔπι: Notice the anastrophe.

Meleager

8

Love's Parentage (*A. P.* 5. 180)

This epigram may be a little mannered for modern tastes, but it is very much in the Alexandrian style. Within the limits of Meleager's intent, the conceit is neatly turned and the language at times startling. Water and flame appear once again, as in Selection 6.

1 Τί ξένον: "What is so strange...?" τόξα, in view of the verb which follows, must be translated as "arrows".

2 λαμυροῖς: Although the word means "hungry" or "wanton", it is tempting to see in Eros' eyes some trace of the lynx-glance encountered in Selection 7.

3 στέργει: Contrary to Liddell-Scott-Jones, the verb often implies sexual attraction.

4 κοινά: "common property".

6 Although Eros has a mother and a grandmother, he has (according to Meleager) no father or paternal grandfather. Others suggest that his father was Ares, Zeus, Hermes, or Chaos.

7-8 Eros, therefore, embodies those very manifestations which are seen in lovers.

9

Manus Manum Lavat (*A. P.* 5. 208)

The theme is treated elsewhere by Meleager (Selection 94) as well as in a paederestic apology (Selection 18) and by Asclepiades (*A. P.* 12. 17).

2 ἀνδροβατεῖν: "to have anal intercourse".

3-4 ἁ χεὶρ γὰρ τὰν χεῖρα: Cf. *inter alia* Petronius 45. 13 (*computa, et tibi plus do quam accepi. Manus manum lavat*). The remainder of the couplet is unintelligible. Such emendations as καλά με μένει have been suggested, but they have little meaning, especially when ἀρσενικαῖς λαβίσιν, a dative, should but cannot mean "along with your mannish embraces". λαβίς: "holder", "clamp", "tongs".

10

Tumultuous Love (*A. P.* 5. 212)

With the quiet intrusion of the little word αἰεί the reader is introduced to some of Meleager's most effective epigrams, those which have as their theme the vision of love as a spiritual or transcendent experience, even to the point of obsession. In this epigram love enters the poet's eyes and ears and penetrates to the essence of his being.

2 The image of a silent, reverential offering expressed here is quite effective. "My eyes in silence bring their tribute of sweet tears to Desire" (Paton).   τὸ: perhaps, "this".

3 ὑπὸ φίλτρων: "from love spells".

4 τύπος: An effective word, since it means both "image" and "impact" or "blow". It is not clear whether the image is of the beloved or of Eros.

5 μὴ καί ποτ᾽: "and perhaps".

6 οὐδ᾽ ὅσον: "not in the least".

11

A Votive Lamp (*A. P.* 6. 162)
This couplet is one of two of Meleager's epigrams included in the "dedicatory" portion of the *Anthology* (Book 6). The epigram is given an amatory turn.

1 Ἄνθεμά = ἀνάθημα: "votive offering".

2 μύστην: "an initiate".   θέτο: "dedicates".

12

The Musicianly Grasshopper (*A. P.* 7. 195)
Meleager introduces an erotic strain into a sub-genre of poetry (epitaphs for animals) which is usually sepulchral. See R. B. Egan, "Two Complementary Epigrams of Meleager (*A. P.* VII, 195 and 196)," *JHS* 108 (1988) 24-32.

1 ἀπάτημα: "deceiver of my passion", since the grasshopper distracts the lover from his thoughts of love.   παραμύθιον ὕπνου: "encouragement to sleep".

3-4 The poem is filled with felicitous Meleagrian phrases: αὐτοφυὲς μίμημα λύρας is one, λάλους πτέρυγας another.   κρέκε means both to "stroke" an instrument, as a musician would, and to "rustle" as a grasshopper would, and so proves to be a splendidly metaphorical word.

5 παναγρύπνοιο: "totally sleepless", a genitive.

6 ἐρωτοπλάνον: "causing to wander".

7 γήτειον: *allium cepa*, a horned onion or perhaps a leek.   ὀρθριvὰ: "in the morning"; adverbial, as often.

8 σχιζομένοις (for σχιζομένας), a reading suggested by Gow

Meleager

and supported by G. Giangrande, "Trois epigrammes de l'Anthologie," *REG* 81 (1968) 47-50: "for your forked tongue."

13
The Midday Reveller (*A. P.* 7. 196)

Once again a noisy insect is called on to distract a lover. A. La Penna ("Marginalia et hariolationes philologae," *Maia* 5 [1952] 110-11) has suggested that this "scene" was was written with Plato in mind (*Phdr.* 229-230). For a "structuralist" interpretation of this epigram see P. Claes, "Close-reading van een Grieks gedicht," *Lampas* 2. 3 (1970) 207-27, and J. P. Guépin's rebuttal, "Een uniek stuk," *Lampas* 3. 3 (1971) 214-28.

1 Ἀχήεις = Ἠχέεις. Cicadas traditionally feed on dewdrops. Here intoxication with such liquid loosens the small creature's "tongue".

2 ἐρημολάλον: "chattering in the wilderness".

3-4 Meleager confuses the functions of grasshoppers with cicadas, which vibrate a membrane in their thorax to produce a shrill sound. **αἰθίοπι** = αἰθός + ὄψ.

5 δενδρώδεσι: "woodland".

6 ἀντῳδὸν κέλαδον: Responsive instrumental playing was as much a part of the bucolic *topos* as amoebaean verse. In amoebaean contests the opening couplet of one competitor is challenged by a couplet extemporized by his rival, who must use the same theme but must demonstrate some intensification, extension, or ludicrous application of it.

7-8 The poet once more seeks sleep as an escape from the torments of love. Sleep at midday is a bucolic theme. The drone of the cicada lulls men and beasts to sleep, but the cicada, still dew-drunk, is the only one to remain awake.

14
The Flame and the Moth (*A. P.* 5. 57)

A terse, economical epigram in which Eros is reminded that the poet's soul is also winged and, if too often burned, will fly away. The epigram is lent pungency by the broad meaning of ψυχή (enthusiasm, consciousness, all consuming love, life).

1 περινηχομένην: "fluttering about".   **πολλάκι**: "over and over".

2 The subject of **φεύξετ'** is supplied from **ψυχήν**.

15

Love at Play (*A. P.* 12. 47)

Eros plays at dice. This is an oft-repeated theme in Greek litera-
ture (see Anacreon fr. 14; Apollonius Rhodius 3. 114 ff.; Antipater
of Sidon, *A. P.* 7.427; Asclepiades, *A. P.* 12. 46). Dice are an appro-
priate symbol for love.

16

Burned Out (*A. P.* 12. 48)

Once again we are treated to a vision of the vanquished lover.
The disappointed suitor, hurled to the ground in a wrestling
match with love, feels himself reduced to a heap of cold ashes. The
metaphor moves from that of wrestling to that of fire. For an epi-
gram similar in theme, see Asclepiades, *A.* P. 12. 166.

2 ναὶ μὰ θεούς: "yes, by heaven".

17

Shun Love's Slavery (*A. P.* 12. 80)

Epigrams in the form of spirited monologues or dialogues are
common in Meleager. Here we find him exhorting his ψυχή which
is about to fall in love again. It is a common *topos*, in this case
enlivened in the hexameter lines by short phrases and interjec-
tions. Meleager introduces a new metaphor in each couplet. For
other treatments of this motif, see Selections 68 and 86.

1 πεπανθὲν: a medical term, as of a "ripened" tumor, but here
used metaphorically.

3 πρός σε Διός: "By Zeus [I beg] you".

18

Questa o quello (*A. P.* 12. 86)

For the subject matter of this monologue, see Selection 9 as
well.

1-2 The contrast of emotions is interesting: Aphrodite incites
men with the fire of passion for women, but Eros drives them like
horses to men.

3-4 Aphrodite would support the choice of boys, not because
she favors her son, but because she is attracted to them as well.

19

A Drunken Monologue (*A. P.* 12. 117)

Another monologue, this one artfully constructed of short out-
bursts between a man's drunken self and his more sober half.
Scholars disagree on the distribution of the parts, but the text
used here follows that suggested by Gow and Page. The epigram is
a κῶμος, a revel with music and dancing which often ended in
parading through the streets.

1 Βεβλήσθω κύβος: a phrase more familiar in the Latin *aleam
iacere*, but here suggesting the chance nature of love's attachments
as well as the idea that the first step should be taken. **Βεβλήσθω** is a
perfect passive imperative. **ἅπτε**: "light the torch". A torch is a lit-
erary requisite for a nighttime assault on a beloved's house.

2 τίν' ἔχεις φροντίδα: The translation of this phrase determines
the allocation of lines in the epigram. With the punctuation
offered here, it should mean, "What do you have in mind?"

4 Ποῦ δ' ἡ πρόσθε λόγων μελέτη: "Where is your former practice
of logic?"

20

I Shall Put Up With Your Daring (*A. P.* 12. 119)

In this conventional poem the sequence of thought is a little dif-
ficult to follow. The lover seeks to drown his torment in wine but,
since wine inflames the passions, he feels himself once more
enkindled.

1 μὰ σέ: "I swear it by you yourself".

5-6 Two angry lines in which the poet accuses Bacchus of
betrayal, since he insists on concealing the particulars of his own
mysteries, yet loosens the tongues of lovers and reveals their
secrets.

21

Love's Slave (*A. P.* 12. 132a)

This and the following epigram appear as one entry in the *Greek
Anthology*. Most editors agree that they are separate poems.

2 The image is that of a birdcatcher who regularly snared small
birds by smearing holly or mistletoe gum on the branches and
twigs. See, for example, the well-known *Bird Catcher Cup* (560-530
B.C.) in the Louvre (G. M. A. Richter, *Greek Art*, 3rd ed. [London

1963] 300).

4 σπαίρεις: "wriggle".

5 If Eros were sympathetic, he would sprinkle the fainting lover with water, but the perfumes he administers only serve to arouse his victim more.

22

Love's Agony (*A. P.* 12. 132b)

3-4 These lines are most suggestive to students of ancient literature, recalling perhaps Thetis' exclamation τέκνον, τί κλαίεις; (*Il.* 1. 362), as well as the passage in the *Aeneid* when Dido fondles Cupid in the form of Ascanius on her lap (*Aen.* 1. 717-719). On the more humorous level, the second half of line 4 (οὐκ ἤδεις ὡς ἐπὶ σοὶ τρέφετο) reminds us of Aesop's Γεωργὸς καὶ ὄφις (Halm 97, Ch. 82) in which the snake λαθὼν ὑπὸ κόλπου κατέθετο.

8 ὀπτῷ μέλιτι: An imaginative alternative to expressions such as "bitter sweet". Honey is a frequent ingredient of Meleagrian verse.

23

One Last Gasp (*A.* P. 5. 197)

A rather undistinguished epigram whose first four lines lack the succinct phrasing characteristic of Meleager. The lover, while confessing that he has experienced a multitude of delights and a variety of girls, admits that he can still manage a few more.

3 φίλα παίγνια: "love play".

4 τέλη: "rites".

24

A Multitude of Girls (*A.* P. 5. 198)

This epigram is a more successful treatment than Selection 23 (*A. P.* 5. 197). For the first time we meet Heliodora, who is central to many of Meleager's most successful poems.

1 οὐ = οὐ μά.

3 βοώπιδος 'Αντικλείας: The adjective is rather startling, since Meleager seldom uses Homeric allusions. This seems to be a sly thrust at tradition: the name of Anticleia, the old nurse of Odysseus, evokes a Homeric epithet, even though Homer's Anticleia would certainly lack the allurements of Meleager's companion.

5 There is a lacuna of approximately eight letters which has never satisfactorily been filled, nor need it be, since the sense is satisfactory. πτερόεντας: another Homeric epithet.

25

Asclepias! (*A. P.* 5. 156)
A splendid little conceit on the charms of Asclepias.

1-2 Γαλήνης: In this context it is perhaps a proper name, but in regular usage the word means "calm sea". The customary expression is ἐλαύνειν γαλήνην, "to sail through calm". Meleager, always inventive of words and felicitous turns, moves from simile to metaphor and suggests that Asclepias invites everyone with her bright glance "to set sail on oceans of love".

26

Chilly Sabbaths (*A. P.* 5. 160)
1 ὑπόχρωτα: "naked".

3 εἰ δέ...πόθος: "if your beloved is a Sabbath-observer". But H. Jacobson ("Demo and the Sabbath," *Mnemosyne* 30, Fasc. 1 [1977] 71-72) suggests that the appropriate time for sexual relations mandated by rabbis for a pious and scholarly man was on the Sabbath, that is, on Saturday. Thus Meleager (who was from Palestine and lived in a partially Semitic culture) applies the word σαββατικὸς to the appropriate time for enjoying the pleasures which Demo has to offer, giving the meaning "the sexual desire which is characteristic of the Sabbath".

4 ψυχροῖς: perhaps in both the physical and metaphorical sense.

27

Linger, Night! (*A. P.* 5. 172)
The *topos* is an old one going back to Sappho (see A. T. Hatto, *Eos, An Enquiry Into the Theme of Lovers' Meetings and Partings at Dawn in Poetry* [London, The Hague, Paris 1965]). It is an *aubade*, a morning song.

1 δυσέραστε: "enemy of lovers".

2 ἄρτι...χλιαινομένῳ: "just now warming myself in Demo's arms", suggesting that the poet, rather than having spent the entire night with Demo, has just arrived.

4 The antithesis of γλυκὺ and πικρότατον is somewhat labored but poetically effective.   φῶς...πικρότατον: "as one casting on me a bitter light" (J. Moore-Blunt).

5-6 ἐπ' Ἀλκμήνην...ἀντίος: "You came head on toward Zeus as far as Alcmene" (J. Moore-Blunt, "Two Epigrams by Meleager," *Emerita* 46 [1978] 87). Moore-Blunt suggests that Alcmene sits astraddle Zeus, facing him (in a favored position for sexual intercourse), and that the star rising from behind her "came to overhang her (ἐπ' Ἀλκμήνην)". Zeus saw it immediately and sent it back. This is one of the few verses in which Meleager introduces the trappings of standard Greek mythology. The tale of Alcmene is one of genetic miracles found occasionally in Greek lore. While Alcmene's husband Amphitryon was at war, Zeus visited her in her husband's form, protracting the night so he might better enjoy her pleasures. Later Alcmene was delivered on the same day of two sons: the first was Heracles sired by Zeus, the second was Iphicles who had been sired by Amphitryon.

In arriving at dawn, Meleager seems not to be asking for two nights strung together such as Zeus enjoyed, but simply one entire night with Demo.

28

Perversity (*A. P.* 5. 173)
This epigram and the preceding one may be taken as a pair.
1 περὶ κόσμον: "about heaven".
4 ὡς: "as though".   ἐπιχαιρέκακον: "rejoicing in my misfortunes".

29

Zenophila's Allure (*A. P.* 5. 139)
1 ναὶ Πᾶν': "by Pan". Swearing an oath by this traditional deity of Arcadia's glades and mountains lends a bucolic flavor to the epigram.
3 The turn is a clever one: we are usually told of maidens who flee Pan, but here in an Arcadian context the lover seeks to flee his beloved.
4 οὐδ' ὅσον: "not at all".

30
Gifts of the Graces (*A. P.* 5. 140)

Although the meaning is clear, the train of thought is somewhat difficult to follow. The three Graces have endowed Zenophila with musical ability, eloquence, and beauty. Each of these winning characteristics has been presented to her through the appropriate intermediary: the Muses, with their lyre; Logos (the ability to speak) in the company of Persuasion; and Eros accompanied by Beauty. In such a context the Muses make Zenophila the perfect songstress, Logos makes her the persuasive speaker, and love inspired in her lover makes her beautiful. For a summary of the use of the word πείθειν in amatory contexts in Greek literature from Homer to Alexander of Aetolia, see Nicolas P. Gross, *Amatory Persuasion in Antiquity* (Newark, Delaware 1985) 16-19. See, as well, Selection 39 and Callimachus, *A. P.* 5. 145.

1 πηκτίδι: a twenty-stringed Lydian harp. **ἔμφρων**: "sensible, wise".

2 κάλλος ὑφηνιοχῶν: A conjecture by F. Graefe (*Meleagri Gadareni Epigrammata* [Leipzig 1811]) for a meaningless καλὸς ἐφ᾽ ἡνιόχῳ.

31
The Sweet Rose of Persuasion (*A. P.* 5. 144)

The association of Zenophila and meadow flowers is a pleasing trope, especially since nature is frequently viewed with mistrust and suspicion in Greek literature. It is difficult to identify many of the flowers in this text. What, for example, is a κρίνα? A lily, yes; but the species escapes us. Or what is a λευκόιον other than a white flower of some sort? Gow and Page suggest a "snowdrop". Even the narcissus is a flower distinct from the variety we are accustomed to. See as well Selection 45.

1 φίλομβρος: Calling the narcissus "rain loving" implies a freshness in Zenophila's appearance, just as the λευκόιον suggests her clear complexion.

2 οὐρεσίφοιτα: A troublesome word for editors who do not perceive lilies as "mountain wanderers".

4 Ζηνοφίλα Πειθοῦς ἡδὺ ῥόδον: "Zenophila, the sweet rose of persuasion", a startling and extremely attractive phrase.

5 φαιδρά: "joyously".

6 κρέσσων: "preferable to."

32

A Portrait of Zenophila (*A. P.* 5. 149)

Meleager is at his concise best in this epigram of no great originality. The conceit is charmingly conveyed in the last line by δῶρα διδοὺς and by repetition of the word χάρις. See Selections 37 and 47 as well as Callimachus (*A. P.* 5. 146).

1 The poet appears to be speaking of a portrait (ἔργον, δῶρα) of Zenophila. In that case τίς παρέδειξεν would be best translated with the phrase, "What (painter) represented (in painting)...".

4 καὐτὰν...χάριτι: "even the Grace herself in his gracious gift".

33

Buzz Off (*A. P.* 5. 151)

In this ironical phantasy Meleager exhorts some determined mosquitoes to seek sustenance in his own flesh and not in that of his mistress. The commands of the jealous lover to keep hands off his mistress are made more humorous and vivid by the use of parodic language ('Οξυβόαι, σίφωνες αἵματος, κνώδαλα διπτέρυγα, θῆρες ἄτεγκτοι).

4 ἰδού gives immediacy to the poet's plea.

7 προλέγω: "I warn you".

34

Hercules Minor (*A. P.* 5. 152)

The mosquito appears again, this time in a heroic context: if he succeeds in his mission, he will be awarded the accoutrements of one of mythology's greatest heroes, Heracles. We might assume, then, that his commission is fraught with difficulties and impossible for lowly mortals. But G. Giangrande ("Meleager und die Mücke," *Mnemosyne* 25 [1972] 296-302) suggests an alternative interpretation, reminding us that the summoning of Zenophila would not necessarily require heroic acts, since she is after all an hetaera and so "on call". We should remember, first, that the mosquito in antiquity was topically thought of as *bestia bellicosa* and *gloriae appetens*. Next, we should keep in mind that Eros is frequently referred to as τοξότης and πτερόεις, and thus, like the mosquito, has wings and a stinger; in a splendid example of that *arte allusiva* of which Meleager is master, Eros is dubbed another mosquito. The ironical tone is heightened by the contrast of the diminutive mosquito with the over-sized demi-god Heracles. The humor is well sustained throughout the entire eight lines of the epigram.

See, as well, U. and D. Hagedorn, "Anthologia Palatina V 152 in bildlicher Darstellung," *ZPE* (1983) 61-62, in which they discuss the phrase, ὦ λήθαργε φιλούντων εὕδεις as it appears on a *Steinplatte* found in Egypt and apparently from Roman times.

1 ταχὺς ἄγγελος: A Homeric epithet (*Il.* 24. 292).

2 προσψιθύριζε: a charming onomatopoetic touch, contrasting grotesquely with φιλόμουσε in line 4.

6 κινήσῃς...ὀδύνας: "arouse pangs of jealousy against me in her lover".

35

Zenophila's Garrulous Cup (*A. P.* 5. 171)

The "cup theme" is repeated by Meleager in later epigrams (Selection 43: *A. P.* 5. 137; Selection 84: *A. P.* 12. 133) with numerous variations.

4 ἀπνευστὶ: "without a breath" and so "at one gulp".

36

Slumbering Zenophila (*A. P.* 5. 174)

2 ἄπτερος: "(although) without wings" and so not the true god of sleep. εἰσῄειν: Imperfect optative, first person.

3 ὁ...Διὸς ὄμματα θέλγων: the god Hypnos.

37

Love at Large (*A. P.* 5. 177)

This and the following epigram (*A. P.* 5. 178) serve as public denunciations of Eros. The town crier speaks, describing Love as though he were a run-away animal (or slave). Diatribe finished, he spots the tiny creature circling around its nest or den. We are suddenly made aware that the crier is the poet who has spied Eros huddled many times in the eyes of his beloved. This neatly turned epigram says nothing new, but says all freshly and delightfully. For a similar treatment of the theme, see Moschus' *Idyll* 1.

1 Κηρύσσω τὸν Ἔρωτα τὸν ἄγριον: "I proclaim that Eros is on the rampage".

3 ἀθαμβής: "fearless".

4 σιμὰ γελῶν: "smirking".

5 οὐκέτ' ἔχω φράζειν: "I cannot go on to say".

7-8 The conceit of these two lines is appropriate, but mythology allows that Eros had at least Aphrodite for a mother and a battery of possible fathers. See Selection 8 (*A. P.* 5. 180), note to line 6.

8 λίνα: The image is reversed, since humans, to protect themselves, should seek to trap the little winged creature in nets and not allow him to catch them.

9-10 If Eros has returned to his nest, where has he been? Lost? Inspiring someone else to love? Has he been setting traps in Zenophila's eyes, and is his nest there?

38

Love for Sale (*A. P.* 5. 178)

This charming, striking epigram is much in the style of the previous one. We are given another public repudiation of Eros, this time at the slave market, where the poet as slave dealer describes the characteristics of the infant. They should be "selling points", but they soon reveal the innocent tot as the not-so-innocent God of Love. When the infant begins to practice the tricks of his trade for which he is so infamous, the slaver, rather than seek a purchaser at any price, softens and suggests that Zenophila might rear him.

2 τί δέ μοι: not "What is it to me?", but perhaps "What good is it for me?"

3 σιμὸν: "pug-nosed".

3-4 ἄκρα δ' ὄνυξιν κνίζει: A suggestion of love's malignity.

5 πρὸς δ' ἔτι λοιπὸν: "as for the rest". **ἄθρεπτον**: "unnurseable" (Gow and Page). **ὀξὺ δεδορκός**: Another suggestion of malignity.

6 αὐτᾷ ματρὶ φίλα: "very own mother".

7 ἀπόπλους: "off on a journey".

39

Zenophila's Attractions (*A. P.* 5. 195)

This rather unsuccessful epigram uses the same material as Selections 30 and 40.

1 συνεῖραν: An anonymous conjecture (found in Stadtmüller's and Paton's editions) for συνεῦναι of the manuscript. Although the meaning is satisfactory for the context, the form is not encountered elsewhere in the *Greek Anthology*.

3 πόθον is defined by εὐνάν on line 5.

4 ἵμερον is defined by κάλλος on line 6.

40

Further Allurements (*A. P.* 5. 196)

See Selections 30 and 39 for a variation of this theme.

1 σύγκοιτα φίλτρα: We must assume that the "charms of love as bed companions" connote "know-how".

41

A New Love (*A. P.* 5. 24)

This epigram is attributed in the *Greek Anthology* to Philodemus, but because of the infrequency of the name Heliodora in non-Meleagrian portions of the *Anthology* (5. 125; 11. 256) it is now widely accepted as Meleager's. Neither its place in the *Anthology* nor its language offers clues to its authorship.

1 προλέγει: "warns".

3-4 ἡ ἀναιδής αὐτή: That is, its ψυχή.

42

A Toast (*A. P.* 5. 136)

This epigram is modelled on Callimachus, *A. P.* 12. 51. The jilted lover makes a pathetic toast to the unfaithful Heliodora. The wine should not be mixed with water but—as appropriate—with the name of the beloved, Heliodora.

1 Ἔγχει: "Pour out", and so "Fill up the cup". Ἡλιοδώρας: Genitive of the person toasted: "Here's to Heliodora".

2 ἀκρήτῳ: "unmixed [wine]".

5 φιλέραστον: Used, as often in Meleager, to mean "sympathetic to lovers" or "enhancing lovers".

43

A Second Toast (*A. P.* 5. 137)

A variation on the previous epigram.

1-2 "Pour out one for Heliodora-Persuasion and one for Heliodora-Cypris, one again for Heliodora that same sweet-spoken Grace".

3-4 γράφεται might mean either that the poet writes θεὸς καλός on the walls (see Selection 94, *A. P.* 12. 41), or, more likely, that Heliodora has all the attributes of Peitho, Cypris, and Charis in herself and so "is considered by me the one goddess". Garrison (*Mild Frenzy*, 81) suggests that the poet is saying that his soul suffers from love's thirst and, in somewhat awkward imagery, is suggesting love's internalization as well as its elevation to a holy status. See Selection 35, where Meleager would like Zenophila to drink his heart and soul.

44
The Sweetness of Her Voice (*A. P.* 5. 141)

Throughout Meleager's poetry much is communicated *sotto voce*, whether it concerns bees or gnats or sweethearts. Here it is Heliodora's whispers which are more soothing and more enticing than the music of the gods.

45
Heliodora's Garland I (*A. P.* 5. 143)

This epigram has the same subject matter as the longer version of Selection 46, but the conceit is different. As Gow and Page (drawing on Philostratus, *Ep.* 9) explain, it is not that Heliodora is more beautiful than withered flowers, but that the garland that she is wearing cannot stand the rivalry with her beauty, so that on contact with her brow it fades away and dies.

46
Heliodora's Garland II (*A. P.* 5. 147)

A luxuriant epigram, simple in style. For earlier use of many of these flowers, see Selection 31.

4 φιλέραστα: See Selection 42. 5.

5-6 "So that the garland may wrap its entwining foliage about the temples of sweet-tressed Heliodora".

47
Heliodora's Immortality (*A. P.* 5. 148)

1 ἐν μύθοις: "in people's conversations".

2 The playful use of Χάριτας χάρισιν by now has become a commonplace in Meleager: see Selections 30 and 32.

Meleager

48
Heliodora's Embrace (*A. P.* 5. 155)
This motif is repeated later in Selections 110 and 111.

49
The Savage Scratch (*A. P.* 5. 157)
The point of this little poem hinges on the meaning of κνίσμα in the second line. Basically it means "that which is caused by itching" and so a "scratch". But here we are dealing with pleasurable stimulation.

1 ἀνέτραφες: "trained by".

2 κνίσμα: "tickling". Compare Selection 38, note to 3-4, and Selection 67.

50
A Bee in the Bonnet (*A. P.* 5. 163)
We meet again one of the small winged animals (reminiscent of Erotes) of which Meleager is so fond. The poem is a fresh treatment of an old subject, but is marred by what appears to be a confusion of images, and by inconsistency between lines 1-2 and the remainder of the poem. Why, for example, in the context of the remaining lines, does the bee attack Heliodora? At the outset we would imagine that the tiny creature, nurtured on flowers, has been turned into a raging monster or a jealous lover by Heliodora's charms. Or perhaps, as a bee, it seeks to extract Heliodora's sweetness as if she were a blossom. But that turns out not to be the case; we are told rather that she has both the sweetness and the bitter venom of love in her heart, so that she resembles the bee who seeks sweets but harbors a sting as well.

3 δύσοιστον is out of place in the context. It presents metrical problems, and attempts at emendation (the most popular is δυσύποιστον) result in a clumsy phrase (δυσύποιστον πικρὸν κέντρον) uncharacteristic of Meleager. An adverb seems called for.

5 φιλέραστε: "friendly to [this] lover", since the bee has warned him of Heliodora's nature.

51
A Second Endymion (*A. P.* 5. 165)
In this effective epigram the poet beseeches Night as his cham-

pion to lull his rival to sleep in Heliodora's arms and keep her faithful (if not pure) for him. See Asclepiades, *A. P.* 5. 7.

1 Ἓν τόδε: "this one thing".

2 πότνια Νύξ: In this phrase our predictably parodic poet addresses Night as though in serious prayer.

4 ὑπναπάτῃ: It is usually jealousy which this adjective describes as "sleep-robbing"; but here Heliodora's σύγκοιτα φίλτρα (see Selection 40) are at work.

5 κοιμάσθω μὲν λύχνος: Lovers in their intoxication with one another would keep a lamp lit, but the poet, seeking everything conducive to sleep and to Heliodora's abstinence, asks that night snuff out the lamp.

6 The verbs (ῥιπτασθεὶς and [line 3] βεβλημένος) are remarkably violent. We suppose that the poet wishes his rival to become permanently inactive. According to the myth, Selene, the moon, becoming enamoured of Endymion, passed her nights in his company and neglected her obligations. When she appeared toward morning, she was even paler and more fatigued than usual because of her nocturnal activities. Zeus, discovering the affair, gave Endymion a choice between death in whatever way he wished or eternal sleep and beauty. Endymion chose the latter, and as William Basse recalls in his *Urania*:

> Erronious Fame reports that she hath kept
> Him ever since within her spotlesse sphere.

52

Heliodora's Fidelity (*A. P.* 5. 166)

These eight lines appear to plunge deep into the consciousness of the poet as he speaks of his hope for intimacy in Heliodora's thoughts.

2 σκολιῶν ὄρθρων defies emendation. **δακρυχαρῆ:** "welcoming tears".

3 στοργῆς ἐμὰ λείψανα: An hypallage, that is, "a change in the relation of words by which a word, instead of agreeing with the case it logically qualifies, is made to agree grammatically with another case" (Smyth, *Greek Grammar*, p. 678).

4 ψυχρᾷ...ἐν εἰκασίᾳ: "on my cold picture". There are a number of references in ancient literature to images or pictures of one's beloved (e.g. Strato, *A. P.* 12. 183; Propertius 4. 7. 47-48). The validity of Graefe's conjecture (εἰκασίᾳ) is defended by E. K. Borthwick ("Meleager's Lament: A Note on *Anth. Pal.* 5. 166," *CPh* 64 (1969) 173-75.

5 κἀμὸν: "for me".

6 ψυχαπάτην: "beguiling" and "deluding".

7 νέα παίγνια: "a new lover [plaything]".

8 ἧς παρέδωκα: Gow and Page suggest ὧν instead of ἧς, pointing out that assimilation to ἧς would have been quite easy after ἐσίδῃς, εἴης, and that the meaning of ὧν ("Be watchful over those things I entrust to you"), referring to the poet's own amours, would give a much better meaning.

53

Heliodora's Sporting (*A. P.* 5. 214)

The conceit that a lover's heart is a ball is both novel and slightly distasteful to modern audiences. The epigram itself is concise and in the Meleagrian tradition.

2 παλλομέναν κραδίαν: "my bouncing heart".

3 Πόθον here stands for Eros.

3-4 εἰ δ' ἀπὸ σεῦ με ῥίψαις: "if you throw me aside".

4 ἀπάλαιστρον: "unsportsman-like".

54

I Beseech You, Love (*A. P.* 5. 215)

While this epigram is ascribed to Posidippus in the *Planudean Anthology*, in Book 5 of the *Palatine Anthology* it is ascribed to Meleager and set in a Meleagrian context. Its style favors Meleagrian authorship as well.

2 κοίμισον: "lull to sleep". **μοῦσαν ἐμὰν ἱκέτιν:** "my humble petition".

6 μιαιφονίαν: "murderous character" (Gow and Page).

55

Kidnapped (*A. P.* 12. 147)

Even though there seems to be no satisfactory solution to the garble of the first line, this little poem is vivid, original in concept, and witty.

56

An Elegy for Heliodora (A. P. 7. 476)

Meleager takes on a somber tone. For an extended discussion of the epigram see Stuart G. P. Small, "The Composition of *Anth. Pal.* VII, 476 (Meleager)," *AJPh* 72 (1951) 47-56.

4 A striking and effective line. "I pour them out as a libation of longing, in memory of affection" (Peter Jay).

5 καὶ ἐν φθιμένοις: "even among the dead", a common phrase.

7 τὸ ποθεινὸν ἐμοὶ θάλος: "the warmth I desire".

8 ακμαῖον δ' ἄνθος ἔφυρε κόνις: Another striking phrase.

9-10 These lines have been criticized as dull; but a retreat into homely remarks and clichés is to be expected in dealing with death, and so perhaps adds a sincere ring to the earlier verses.

57

Callistion's Charms (A. P. 5. 192)

A play on words which is always refreshing.

2 "The double letter of the Syracusans has been changed [from χ to τ]". The Syracusan double letter is χ. We cannot ascertain why it is called a double letter unless the Syracusans were believed to pronounce ἰσχίον as "isc-hion". Pliny in his *Natural History* (7. 56) tells us that Epicharmus, the chief comic poet among the Dorians, who spent the later years of his life at the court of Hieron in Syracuse, added both χ and θ to the Greek alphabet.

58

Common Coin (A. P. 5. 187)

1 Dorcas appears to be either a slave of Lycaenis or her procuress.

1-2 ὡς ἐπίτηκτα φιλοῦσα ἥλως: "how while kissing you have been caught as a counterfeit". ἐπίτηκτα means "melted on" and so "counterfeited".

2 πλαστόν: "counterfeit".

59

Timarion's Lipstick (A. P. 5. 96)

This clever epigram displays Meleager's verbal dexterity. The following epigram (Selection 60) suggests that Timarion (whether a real or literary figure) was not compliant. Bird lime appears once

Meleager

again (see Selection 21) as a metaphor for the power of a love which binds.

2 Gow and Page point out the chiastic relationship of the first line to the second.

60
Timarion the Scow (*A. P.* 5. 204)

The comparison of prostitutes to ships which should be in mothballs is a time-honored theme going back at least as far as Alcaeus (Lobel and Page, *Poetarum Lesbiorum Fragmenta*, frag. 306. 14. ii). See as well Asclepiades, *A. P.* 5. 161.

This epigram is noteworthy for the difficulty which its expression and vocabulary causes for modern readers. Many consider it the nadir of Meleager's art; but its determined anti-feminism makes it an instructive document and a mine for obscene innuendo.

1 Timarion is the subject of the sentence. τὸ πρὶν γλαφυροῖο κέλητος: We must assume, since Timarion is called a "slick corsair", that she had not only been somewhat of a beauty in her heyday but had also been adept at sailing away with other people's money.

2 πλωτὸν: perhaps best taken as an adverb, "under sail".

3 ἐπὶ νώτοισι μετάφρενον: "the middle of your back". From this we would gather that she is hunchbacked from pushing upward too much.

4 πολιὸς δ' ἐκλέλυται πρότονος: "your old grey forestay is slack", a meaningless phrase which has not been elucidated by editors. πολιὸς could mean hair, but that meaning always requires the plural. πρότονος has been interpreted as "spine", but most conjectures are far from satisfactory.

5 ἰστία...μαστῶν: "your drooping breasts hang down like flapping sails".

6 Timarion is the subject.

7 πάνθ' νεώς = πάντα τὰ τῆς νεώς. This and the following verse contain quite unattractive anatomical descriptions.

8 γόνασιν...σάλος: It appears that Timarion has a sailor's gait, one of the unfortunate physical manifestations of her profession.

9 δύστανος τίς ζωὸς: Gow and Page's suggestion for this passage. It appears to give the sense needed.

10 εἰκοσόρου: If Timarion is "twenty-oared", either corpulence

78

has been added to the characteristics of her old age, or, in the metaphorical sense, she is capable of taking on twenty lovers in a working day. It has been suggested, quite legitimately, that εἰκό-σορον contains an additional sense of τὸ σορῷ ἐοικός (coffin-like), since σορός may stand for "old woman" (Athenaeus, *Deipnosophistae* 13. 580c).

61

Timarion's Conquest (*A. P.* 12. 109)

Timarion appears, we must imagine, in her salad days. We are offered a novel variation of a paederastic epigram in which the ἐρόμονος is enamoured of a hetaera.

62

Timarion in Her Prime (*A. P.* 12. 113)

Timarion's supreme conquest is of Eros himself. The use of hunting vocabulary perhaps implies that she knows him for the dangerous wild beast he really is.

63

Delicacy Incarnate (*A. P.* 5. 154)

Tryphera's beauty is compared to that of Aphrodite at the moment she was born from the froth of the sea. (See A. Wifstrand, *Studien zur Griechischen Anthologie* [Lund 1926] 72.)

1 We are reminded of Apelles' famous *Aphrodite Anadyomene*, and of the epigrams of Leonidas of Tarentum (*A. Pl.* 182) and of Antipater of Sidon (*A. Pl.* 78).

2 Τρυφέρα τρυφερά: So patent a pun, but difficult to reproduce convincingly in English.

64

Love At Sea (*A. P.* 5. 190)

This pleasing epigram concerns the common topic of the gale which sweeps lovers off their feet.

4 τρυφερὴν Σκύλλαν: Translate the oxymoron as "our delicate Scylla", keeping in mind that we are still speaking of the hetaera Tryphera in Selection 63. See also Selections 93 and 119.

65

Phanion's Hare (*A. P.* 7. 207)

Another mock-heroic epigram on a tiny animal. The *Palatine Anthology* contains a number of such epitaphs for animals (see especially those of Anyte [*A. P.* 7. 190, 202, 208, 215]). They are often in a more serious vein: see *A. P.* 9. 86 (Antiphilus of Byzantium)—the mouse that tried to eat an oyster and was eaten by the oyster instead. Only here does an animal achieve immortality through its stomach. The humor is typical, we imagine, of Meleager's Menippean satire.

1-4 The length of the sentence, running through two complete couplets and introducing the subject near the end, adds solemnity to the first part of the epitaph. It is disconcerting to discover shortly afterwards that the hare's demise was the result of gluttony.

7 κλισίᾳ: "bed".

66

Phanion Waits (*A. P.* 12. 53)

It has been suggested that this epigram reflects an actual occasion in the poet's life, but that need not be so. Apostrophes to ships are not uncommon in ancient poetry (see, for example, Catullus *c.* 4).

1 Εὔφορτοι: Gow and Page suggest that "well-freighted" would be a peculiar word to use of ships if Meleager's experience were not first-hand. Yet it is a new formation, as is πελαγίτιδες, and so characteristic of the elegant adjectives which our *poeta doctus* customarily compounds. εὔφορτοι, καλὸν, κόλποις, χαροπὸν (line 4), and καλαὶ (line 5) establish a romantic and erotic mood for the poem. πόρον Ἕλλης: the Hellespont.

2 κόλποις: "folds of the sail".

3 Κῴαν κατὰ νᾶσον: "in the region of the island of Cos".

5 κομίζει: "escort".

6 The poet is a practical ancient traveller, preferring to journey as much as possible by land. For that reason, instead of sailing directly from the Hellespont, he will come by land through the Troas, Mysia, Aeolis, Ionia and Caria, and then cross over to Cos by sea from Halicarnassus.

67

Love Rekindled I (*A. P.* 12. 82)

In this and the following epigram (*A. P.* 12. 83) the poet plays on the name of Phanion, his mistress.

2 Apparently the Phoenix is not the only thing born from its ashes.

3 χερὸς δ' ἀκρώνυχα δισσά: "his two finger tips", the thumb and the index finger.

4 κνίσμα πυρὸς: Gow and Page suggest "a pinch of fire"; but the phrase also means the "itch of passion", a condition requisite for the rekindling of a love affair. See Selection 49 (*A. P.* 5. 157).

68

Love Rekindled II (*A. P.* 12. 83)

This epigram reworks the preceding one.

5-6 Editors are troubled by the antithesis between βραχὺ φανίον and πῦρ ψυχῆς. Meleager certainly intended the latter expression to denote overwhelming passion (as opposed to a tiny flame). The phrase is elliptical as are many in Meleager, and the term πῦρ ψυχῆς, although not startlingly new, is arresting.

69

Broken Promises (*A. P.* 5. 8)

The attribution of this epigram is uncertain, since it is ascribed to Philodemus in the *Planudean Anthology*, but appears in the *Palatine Anthology* in a Meleagrian context. On the other hand, we have no extant epigrams by Meleager in which a woman is speaker, whereas there are several such by Philodemus. This could possibly be a paederastic epigram, but the use of the lamp motif and the expression ἐν κόλποις is much more common in heterosexual contexts.

4 κοινὴν...μαρτυρίην: "Common to both of us was the testimony you received" (Page).

5 ὅρκιά...φέρεσθαι: This phrase strikes a response in lovers of Catullus (*c.* 70) and Callimachus (*A. P.* 5. 6), but it is quite a common trope in earlier Greek literature. Plato and Menander are the better known of those writers employing it.

Meleager

70

A Perjured Oath (*A. P.* 5. 175)

This excellent epigram is in Meleager's elaborate style, adorned with a number of new or otherwise unattested adjectives.

1 μοι κενὸς ὅρκος: "Your oath, alas for me, is broken (empty, meaningless)".

4 σφιγκτὸς...μίτος: "the tightly fastened binding threads for garlands about your temples".

8 χειροτυπὴς πάταγος: Although moderns associate castanets with Spain, they are common throughout the Mediterranean world.

71

Dorcas on the Run (*A. P.* 5. 182)

This lively epigram demonstrates Meleager's talent for encapsulating the spirit of the mime within the modest limits of an epigram. The style is straightforward and vivacious; and the episode is capped by a clever twist in the last couplet.

1 We have met Dorcas as a go-between before (Selection 58, *A. P.* 5. 187).

3 βραχύ...ἐπίσχες: "Just a minute, please, Dorcas, hang on just a minute".

7 A number of superficially acceptable emendations have been made to this line (σὺ τὰ πάντα λέγειν, δεῖ πάντα λέγειν), but Gow and Page have found them unacceptable on stylistic grounds. The meaning is clear.

8 καὐτὸς: "I, myself".

72

Love's Prisoner (*A. P.* 5. 184)

This is another example of Meleager's abilities in writing mime. The poet, jealous of his mistress' supposed infidelities, threatens to keep her at his side so that she cannot visit her new lover. The punishment promised in the final line, though ingenious, is somewhat strained.

1 τί θεούς: "Why implore the gods?".

4 νῦν νῦν ἔτι: "even now".

5 περίβλεπτός: "handsome".

6 κακὸν κοίτης θηρίον: "wicked bed-bug".

7-8 Meleager thinks to send her packing, but in the second half of the pentameter changes his mind: "Remain here just as you are, my prisoner".

73
A Suppliant's Flowers (*A. P.* 5. 191)
With a technique now familiar, Meleager combines the theme of *exclusus amator* with a dedicatory epigram (lines 9-10). The lover walks to his mistress' house imagining the reception she has in store for him. His conclusion is melancholy.

2 σύμπλανον: "companion". ὀργάνιον: The type of instrument eludes us. It is a small one, appropriate to a serenade. A flute? A mandolin?

4 Since the girl is accustomed to light her lamp while awaiting her lover, her amorous anticipation is described in terms of a lamp: "totally consumed by the desire kindled by her lamp".

5 μαράνθας: The poet's tears continue the image of the lamp: they were "burning" and so withered the flowers.

7-8 ὁ μύστης σῶν κώμων: "the devotee of your revels". στοργᾶς: "passionate love".

74
Triple Fire (*A. P.* 9. 16)
The poet exclaims that he is in love with three women at once. The two couplets are somewhat strained and the epigram marred by a corruption which has not been satisfactorily emended. The subject of the verb κατήρισεν must be Eros, but it is not expressed. It has been suggested that Ἔρως be substituted for τοι, but it is impossible to see how such a corruption could have taken place.

75
Hail, Morning Star (*A. P.* 12. 114)
This fine and neatly phrased epigram apostrophizes the Morning Star to return soon in the guise of the Evening Star and to bring with it the poet's mistress whom it takes away at dawn.

76
A Multitude of Boys (*A. P.* 12. 94)
The poet invites Philocles to pander all of the young men he

Meleager

would like, but to keep his distance from Myiscus, the poet's favorite. For other epigrams on Myiscus, see Selections 78, 99-108.

1 For Heraclitus, see Selections 78, 90-92.

4 τὸ λειπόμενον: "what is left unsaid", other parts of his anatomy.

5 οἷος ἐμὸς νόος ἄφθονος: "the kind of ungrudging mind I have".

6 λίχνος: "greedily".   **τὸ καλόν**: The phraseology here is awkward; what is needed is τι καλόν.

77

Lanx Satura (*A. P.* 12. 95)

In spite of its lyrical opening, this epigram skitters into the obscenities which send translators off pell mell to their dictionaries searching for terms which will obfuscate the words and actions of the young men who appear in these ten lines. We have met before, or will meet again, many of the actors in this paederastic melée: Diodorus (Selections 61, 76, 78. 91), Dion (Selections 76, 78, 88), Ouliades (Selections 76, 78), Theron (Selection 78).

2 κάλλευς: "of beauty".

5 εὔστοχον: "hitting the mark". We wonder if this refers to his accuracy or his potency.

6 περισκυθίσαι: LSJ translates this as "scalp in the Scythian fashion" in citing use of the phrase in surgical operations, sidestepping its obscene meaning, "to perform fellatio".

10 Ῥωμαϊκὴν λοπάδα: We are speaking, then, of a *lanx satura*, a mixed salad.

78

Meleager's Other Garland (*A. P.* 12. 256)

The mention of a στέφανος at the beginning of this epigram and the association of the boys mentioned in it with flowers have tempted some scholars to believe that this short poem might have either introduced a collection of *Paedica* by Meleager, which was perhaps issued separately and then incorporated into the *Garland* later, or been used as an introduction to a general collection of paederastic poetry. Gow and Page contend that it seems simply to be an epigram about a number of young men.

2 ψυχαπάτην στέφανον should be taken in apposition with Πάγκαρπον παίδων ἄνθος.

4 See Selection 31 (*A. P.* 5. 144) for a discussion of λευκόιον.

5 ὡς ἀπ' ἀκάνθης: perhaps a reference to Heracleitus' humble background.

8 ἑρπύλλου: A creeping thyme shrub which was used in making wreaths (*seryllum*).

10 ἱμερτοὺς ἀρετῆς κλῶνας is to be taken in apposition with ἀειθαλὲς ἔρνος ἐλαίης. ἀρετῆς refers to the quality assigned to the olive when awarded to victorious athletes. Myiscus, who receives the longest complimentary citation in this poem, is mentioned more than any other boy in Meleager's epigrams. The olive spray—indicating the supreme winner—is reserved for him.

79

Love's Encounter (*A. P.* 12. 127)

In this triumph of Meleagrian art, the language is simple, the thought uninvolved, the imagery compelling. Considerable piquancy is achieved in the last couplet, where the feelings of love are internalized and incorporated into the poet's psychic processes, passing from infatuation to obsession.

8 "Imaging in my soul a loveliness which is living fire" (Paton).

80

Honey-Sweet Wine (*A. P.* 12. 164)

This finely worked paederastic epigram features Alexis and Cleobolus (see Selections 97-98 as well), whose love blends them into an intoxicating unity.

2 καὐτὸν ἐόντα καλόν: "being handsome oneself".

81

A Lover's Farewell (*A. P.* 12. 52)

A paederastic farewell in Meleager's simple, economical style. For another charming poem of departure, see Theocritus, *Idyll* 7. 52 ff.

1 Νότος: Since Notus is the appropriate wind to carry someone to Rhodes, Gow and Page suggest that the poem was perhaps written in Tyre. **ὦ δυσέρωτες**: We must assume that the poet addresses others who have been separated from their lovers.

2 Andragathus is not mentioned elsewhere in Meleager's poetry.

3-4 τρὶς...τρὶς...τετράκι should all be viewed as indefinite num-

Meleager

bers; compare the note on Selection 5, line 6.

82
Cypris' Denial (*A. P.* 12. 54)
See Selections 83 and 89 as well as Asclepiades *A. P.* 12. 75 and 77.

2 Antiochus is found also in Selections 83 and 84.

4 εὕρηται: "proves to be".

83
Eros Without Wings I (*A. P.* 12. 78)
1 A chlamys is a short mantle used as an outer garment, frequently of wool, oblong in shape, and of Macedonian origin. It was the dress of youths, travellers, and hunters. It was customary to pass one of its shorter sides around the neck, fasten it with a πόρπη (a brooch), then allow the remainder to hang down the back. But it could be arranged to suit the whim of the wearer, and was at times wrapped around the arm as a shield.

2 The petasus is a flat, broad-brimmed felt hat used extensively for travel. It was one of the distinguishing marks of the ἔφηβος.

84
Ganymede's Rival (*A. P.* 12. 133)
A charming reworking of themes Meleager uses elsewhere (Selections 35, 101 and 102).

1 θέρευς: genitive of "time within which".

3 The legend of Ganymede portrays Zeus' infidelities at their most blatant. According to Homer (*Il.* 20. 232-35), Ganymede, son of Tros, king of Dardania, was carried away by the gods to be a cupbearer in heaven. Later legend, however, lays the blame squarely on Zeus, who assumed the form of an eagle to consummate the abduction (Ovid, *Met.* 10. 155-61). Astronomers identify Ganymede with the constellation Aquarius.

4 καὶ τόδε σοι χείλεσιν οἰνοχοεῖ: "and pours this intoxication from his lips [on your lips?]".

85

Godly Aristogoras (*A. P.* 12. 122)

Rhianus (*A. P.* 12. 121) is the model for this epigram.

4 καίρια: "timely tales". The remainder of the line is a finely turned phrase.

86

Bitter Honey (*A. P.* 12. 81)

The *topos* "bitter honey" is a common one with Meleager; see Selections 1 (line 22), 22, 87, and 107. The epigram is written in Meleager's unadorned style.

1 Ψυχαπάται: "deceiving one's own soul".

3 νίψαι has troubled commentators, but as G. Giangrande ("Die kalte Dusche des Meleagers," *Mus. Hel.* [1986] 52-53) argues, the infinitive is used *in final-konsekutiven Sinne*. The poet asks that his heart be "given a cold shower" to cool its ardor.   **τακείσης**: A form of τήκω.

6 It is preferable to make **πῦρ** the subject of **ψαῦσαι**.

87

Honey's Bitter Sting (*A. P.* 12. 126)

Diophantus is introduced conventionally as the poet's new love.

1 Ἦρκταί: A form of ἄρχω.   **ἀλύων**: "restless".

2 ταύταν: Supply **κραδίας**.

88

Dion's Ascendancy (*A. P.* 12. 128)

2 αἰγιβάτῃ: "goat mounting", in a sexual context.

3 προφῆτι: "mouthpiece".

3-4 μηδὲ...δάφνῃ παρθενίῃ μέλφ': "do not sing to the virgin laurel", that is, to Apollo.

89

Eros Without Wings II (*A. P.* 12. 76)

The poet experiments with the image of a wingless Eros which we have met before in Selection 83. Both poems, as well as Selection 82, are interpretations of Asclepiades (*A. P.* 12. 75):

Εἰ πτερά σοι προσέκειτο, καὶ ἐν χερὶ τόξα καὶ ἰοί,
    οὐκ ἂν Ἔρως ἐγράφη Κύπριδος, ἀλλὰ σύ, παῖς.

and Asclepiades, *A. P.* 12. 77.

2 πυριβλήτους: "striking with fire". **ἀκίδας**: "stinging arrows" would best combine the two meanings of the word.

4 μορφᾶς: "beauty".

90
The Screen of Years (*A. P.* 12. 33)

An aging ἐρόμενος is viewed as his own bulwark against the amorous advances of suitors. For once the object of affection does not entice with his voice or seduce with his words, but repels because of his mature body. See S. L. Tarán, "ΕΙΣΙ ΤΡΙΧΕΣ: An Erotic Motif", *JHS* 105 (1985) 97-98.

1 ὅτ᾽ ἦν ποτε: "when he lived".   **παρ᾽ ἥβην**: "past his prime".

2 δέρρις: "leather covering" or "shield of skin". It is an ingenious metaphor, since the word describes the leather coverings hung over fortifications to defect the arrows and weapons of attackers. Here it is Heraclitus' drooping posterior which fends off his attackers.   **ὀπισθοβάταις**: "those who would take him from behind".

3 μὴ γαῦρα φρυάσσου: "do not sneer disdainfully".

4 ἔστι καὶ φυομένη Νέμεσις: "Nemesis is born as well...".

91
Love's Allurements (*A. P.* 12. 63)

Although the terminology is commonplace ("burning eyes" and "melting rocks"), the contrast is nicely drawn. Heraclitus appeals to the eyes, but Diodorus has inner qualities which make him attractive; and so one boy "radiates" while the other "smolders". See S. L. Tarán, "ΕΙΣΙ ΤΡΙΧΕΣ: An Erotic Motif," *JHS* 105 (1985) 101.

92
Exclusus Amator I (*A. P.* 12. 72)

This poem treats a conventional theme in a fresh way: Meleager sympathizes with Damis who has spent the night outside his lover's door, faint as much from the sight of his beloved as from the exertions of his night-long vigil.

4 βληθεὶς...ἀνθρακιήν: "like wax flung on burning coals", an appositional simile.

93

Rejected Love (*A. P.* 12. 158)

Although treating a common theme, Meleager imbues this epigram with bitterness. He pleads for the friendship of Theocles, but it is apparent that he is grasping at any straw to keep from losing the boy completely.

2 ἁβροπέδιλος: "soft-sandalled", a compound apparently invented by Meleager. It is well chosen for the situation because Love treads softly "though exceedingly strong".   γυμνὸν: "helpless", but also "naked" in keeping with the wrestling terminology used in the remainder of the line.

3 ξεῖνον ἐπὶ ξείνης: "a stranger in a strange land". The phrase adds a sepulchral touch.

4 ἀκλινέος: "steadfast", but the word also extends the wrestling metaphor.

6 ξυνῆς σωφροσύνης: The word σωφροσύνη is somewhat surprising in this context; as Gow and Page suggest, it may be a suitable word to express a "settled relationship".

7 σὲ...δαίμων: "Destiny has ordained you a god".

94

New Horizons (*A. P.* 12. 41)

This cleverly wrought epigram conveys the poet's rejection of homosexual love. It is not without tongue-in-cheek humor, since many of the epigrams in this collection are paederastic. See Selections 9 and 18.

1 γράφεται: The verb may be interpreted as meaning "to count" or "to esteem", but it might also signify that the poet no longer passes his idle moments writing Θήρων καλός on neighborhood walls.

2 δαλὸς: "a burnt-out torch" (Paton).

3 δασυτρώγλων: "with a hairy posterior", presumably.

4 λασταύρων: λάσταυρος is defined by LSJ as an epithet for a κίναιδος, but that does not clarify greatly the meaning of the word, which is connected with the word λάσται (prostitutes).

95

Theron's Power (*A. P.* 12. 60)

This pithy epigram concerns the blinding charms of one of the poet's friends. See Selection 104 for a variation of the same theme.

96

Rash Words (*A. P.* 12. 141)

This psychological nicety immediately reminds English readers of the Shakespearean commonplace, "The lady doth protest too much, methinks" (*Ham.* 3.2. 242). Once again Meleager displays the vigor of his monologues. The language is terse, and the epigram is nicely pointed in the final couplet.

1 Ἐφθέγξω: aorist middle, second person singular. ἃ μὴ θεός: "what not even a god has spoken".

3-4 αὐτὸς ὑπέστης οὐδὲ Διὸς πτήξας: "you stood your ground, not even cowering before Zeus".

97

Love's Pyre (*A. P.* 12. 74)

This artificial pair of couplets introduces sepulchral matter once more into the context of an amatory epigram. The question whether this Cleobulus (who appears only to be a friend) is the same as the Cleobulus of Selections 80 and 98 is probably not worthy of consideration, given our scant knowledge of the extent to which personal experience enters into these highly artificial confections. Those who would like them to be the same person may suppose that the friendly reconciliation which Meleager sought with Theocles (Selection 93) might in this instance have become a reality. Others may wish to view the epigram simply as a variation of Callimachus, *A. P.* 12. 73.

1 Ἦν τι πάθω: "If I die". τὸ γὰρ πλέον: "almost all the time".

2-3 λείψανον...μέθυσον: To dampen the ashes of a lover with wine is most appropriate, insofar as wine helped him to forget his love while he was living. Now it will extinguish the remaining embers of that passion should he die of love.

98

Cleobulus and Sopolis (*A. P.* 12. 165)

1 Since the the poem is based on a conceit on the name of

Meleager, it would seem at first that the proper word to use in line 1 would be μελανόχρους, but that would certainly be less poetic than the **μελίχρους** of the text. The contrast is established without being overly specific. At the same time the suggestion that the beloved's skin is honey-like creates a more affectionate and erotic context. Use of μελανόχρους in the first line would also betray the conceit prematurely.

2 ἀνθοφόροι: "the bloom of love upon them" (Paton), but it might mean simply that they are servants of Aphrodite (Gow and Page).

4 λευκοῦ = ἀργοῦ.

99

First Love I (*A. P.* 12. 23)

This sepulchral epigram is infused with amatory material, a technique we have come to anticipate in Meleager. The poet imagines himself made a prisoner of love, and asks that Eros, the winner, signify his victory by a simple inscription on the beloved's doorway. The setting up of trophies was a universal practice in ancient warfare. The τρόπαιον was composed of arms captured as booty and was erected on the very spot that enemy had turned (τροπεῖν) to flee.

100

Myiscus' Preeminence (*A. P.* 12. 59)

101

Beware of Zeus (*A. P.* 12. 65)

The theme of Ganymede is introduced once again. See as well Selections 102 and 112.

1 Γανυμήδεος ἀκμήν: "Ganymede in his prime", a periphrasis used frequently in Greek.

2 ἔχῃ carries a sexual connotation.

3 πῆ μοι...ἔστιν: "In some way is it possible?"

4 παιδὶ βαλὼν πτέρυγας: "throwing his wings about the boy".

102

Zeus Defied (*A. P.* 12. 70)

In this splendid epigram the poet states that he will stand up to

Zeus. It reaches a climax on line 4 with the words οἶδα παθὼν ἐλεεῖν, a marvel of concise expression. Gow and Page state that this is the only amatory verse in which Zeus is reported as speaking. The epigram is a variation on its predecessor, Selection 101.

5 μυῖα: We must remember that the poet's caution is due to the fact that Zeus appeared as an eagle when he abducted Ganymede. The miniaturization of so cosmic a threat adds charm to the poem.

103

First Love (*A. P.* 12. 101)

The charm of the first three lines has been brilliantly captured by Propertius in the opening lines of the *Monobiblos* (1-4):

> Cynthia prima suis miserum me cepit ocellis
> > contactum nullis ante cupidinibus.
> Tum mihi constantis deiecit lumina fastus
> > et caput impositis pressit Amor pedibus.

Reading both versions only increases one's enjoyment of Meleager and, thanks to Propertius' skills, clarifies his intentions.

1 ἄτρωτον: "never before wounded".

3 φρύαγμα: "arrogance".

5 ὅσον ἀμπνεύσας: "only just breathing" (Page).

6 In the context of the epigram, we must forget about Leda, Europa, Semele, and the galaxy of young ladies whom Zeus seduced, and suppose that the reference here is to Ganymede.

104

Obsession (*A. P.* 12. 106)

The obsession which lurks in the depths of some of Meleager's erotic poetry is made explicit in these four lines, where it affects both his senses and his imaginative faculties. His waking thoughts are dominated by the image of his beloved. See Selection 95 for a treatment of the same theme.

1 τὸ πᾶν: "all in all".

3 πάντα...φαντάζεται: "everything looks to me like him", that is, "At whatever I look, I see him".

3-4 ἆρ'...χάριν: "Do these eyes, then, see only for the purpose of pleasing the soul...?"

105

Dazzling Beauty (*A. P.* 12. 110)

The favorite Myiscus is again introduced in one of Meleager's more successful epigrams, in which the refulgent beauty of the young man is equated with a sudden flash of lightning.

2 ἀνέδειξεν: "made manifest" (Page).

106

Eros' Victim (*A. P.* 12. 144)

This typical Meleagrian epigram, economical and concisely phrased, concludes with one of the fine turns of speech for which he was so famous.

1 φρενολῃστά: "thief of sanity".

2 διφυῆ ταρασὸν...πτερύγων: "the two flat surfaces of your wings".

3 δύσμαχος: "irresistible".

4 παθὼν ἔμαθες: A fine Aeschylean phrase appears in a distinguished context.

107

Sweet Myiscus (*A. P.* 12. 154)

1 τοὔνομ' ἐμοὶ γλυκύς: "sweet to me in respect to your name", although we are not told what makes his name sweet. It appears to be a conventional expression.

3 ἀνιηρός: "causing distress".

108

Winter and Spring (*A. P.* 12. 159)

While this epigram is filled with the customary commonplaces, especially Meleager's insistence on the potency of the eyes in the matters of love, it is permeated by his elegant sense of form.

1 πρυμνήσι': "stern lines".

4 ἐπισκύνιον: "(the skin above the) eyebrows".

109

The Gale of Love (*A. P.* 12. 167)

This nicely turned but undistinguished epigram perpetuates the image of a lover as storm-tossed and carried by the gusts of his passion to his beloved. The elements and the passions are neatly connected by the parallel construction of Χειμέριον...πνεῦμα and χειμαίνει...πνεύσας.

2 ἁρπαστὸν: "swept away".

110

Praxiteles-Eros-Praxiteles (*A. P.* 12. 56)

The conceit of this epigram—that Praxiteles created a famous statue of Eros and that Eros has created a young Praxiteles—is an ingenious one, but the entire epigram is somewhat verbose and repetitious. See Selection 111.

1 Parian marble was the favored medium of Greek and Roman sculptors because of its whiteness and texture. We assume that the poem refers to Praxiteles' famous statue of Eros at Thespiae, which is commemorated by Antipater of Sidon (*A. Pl.* 167).

3 ἔμψυχον: "living".

4 αὐτὸν ἀπεικονίσας: "making a copy of himself".

5 βραβεύῃ: "controls".

6 γῆς...Πόθων: "the Desires of the earth along with those of the immortals".

7 Μερόπων: See Selection 3, note to 4.   **θεόπαιδα**, because the ἐρόμενος Praxiteles was created by Eros.

8 ὑφαγεμόνα: Compound form of ἡγεμών.

111

Today's Praxiteles (*A. P.* 12. 57)

This version of Selection 110 is somewhat more successful. In this epigram Praxiteles the sculptor is said to have sculpted a lifeless statue of Love, but that Praxiteles' ἐρόμενος has created a living love in the heart of the poet. (See A. Wifstrand, *Studien zur Griechischen Anthologie* [Lund 1926] 71.)

2 ἄψυχον μορφῆς τύπον: "a lifeless figure of beauty".

3 ἐνειδοφορῶν: "bringing shape to".   **ἔμψυχα μαγεύων**: "applying magic art to living matter".

4 τριπανοῦργον: "the arch-scamp".

6 μεταρρυθμίσας: "fashioning" or "molding".

112

Charidamus' Beauty (*A. P.* 12. 68)

Meleager asserts that Charidamus ("Joy of People") is fit for

Zeus, not for a mortal, but still prays that he may have one sign of recognition from the boy as he is being wafted to Olympus. That would be a sufficient taste of heaven for the poet. See Selection 101.

3 τί δέ μοι: "What use is it to me...".

4 ἄνταθλον...ἔρωτι: "a rival for victory in love".

7 ὄμμασι νεῦμα δίυγρον: Gow and Page suggest that the image here is excessively artificial and not in Meleager's limpid style. The phrase might be a corruption of ὄμμασι νεῦμα διύγροις.

8 ἀκροθιγές: "gently touching the lips".

10 The last line is terse in the Meleagrian manner, suggesting both that the poet might perhaps experience Charidamus' love and that it would carry him to heaven too.

113

Sweet Oblivion (*A. P.* 12. 49)

The sympotic epigram moves into the realm of the erotic. Many Greek epigrams contend that a suitable dose of wine encourages love-making and that abstinence enables one to control one's impulses. Meleager's conceit appears to be that the fire of passion can be extinguished with pure wine rather than, as one might expect, with water. The epigram is analyzed by G. Giangrande in *L'Épigramme grecque*, Fondation Hardt, Entretiens XIV (Vandoeuvres-Génève 1967) 129 ff.

2 λάθας δωροδότας: "giver of forgetfulness".

3 οἴνας rather than the more frequent masculine οἴνου.

114

The Shipwrecked Lover I (*A. P.* 12. 84)

2 πρωταπόπλουν: "just arrived from a journey".

3-4 This couplet, crucial to an understanding of the poem, is unclear. φλόγα...ἰδεῖν: "as if shining a torch before me, he flashes the lovely beauty of a boy for me to see". Eros is pictured in one of his conventional postures, a torchbearer. At the same time the poet makes it clear that it is not the god's fire which really inspires him, but the beauty of the boy himself. In the next couplet the poet attempts vainly to seize the image but cannot, for he is aware (both physically and emotionally) that his love is an illusion. The whole expression is rather imprecise and unclear, although at the same time evocative.

6 ἀφαρπάζων: "clasp excitedly".

115

The Shipwrecked Lover II (*A. P.* 12. 85)

This reworking, one couplet longer, of Selection 114 has more of the clarity typical of Meleager at his best, but loses the emotive quality of the earlier poem. The progress of thought is clear. The poet, escaping from a sea voyage (or perhaps a storm), complains that he is beset by worse perils. The poem closes with an appeal to by-standers to save him, not from the sea, as one might expect, but from love. The conceit is a bit strained. This and the earlier epigram contain a mixture of sepulchral and amatory themes.

9 ξενίου: an epithet usually reserved for Zeus in his role as savior, but applied here to Eros, certainly with an ironic twist.

116

A Lover's Eyes (*A. P.* 12. 92)

1 παίδων κύνες: "boy-hunting hounds" (Paton).

3-4 The thought appears to be that the eyes (usually captivated by love) have instead captured a new love (or Eros himself). Such an act is as foolish as sheep capturing a wolf, or a crow a scorpion, or ashes rekindling fire. The final item in the elaboration seems out of place, but satisfies a need in the emotional context of the poem, since the conceit of the epigram is the kindling of love and the roasting of a lover.

5-6 The ψυχή instructs the eyes to do what they will, and then asks why they betray it and run off to the ἱκέτην. To make ἱκέτην a proper name seems a little forced, since Hicetas does not appear in any other of Meleager's epigrams. ἱκέτην should perhaps be translated "to the one who supplicates", that is, to Eros. (See G. Giangrande, "Three Alexandrian Epigrams," *CR* 17 [1967] 128-31.) νενοτισμένα: "damp".

117

Phantasies (*A. P.* 12. 125)

Lover's dreams are not uncommon stock in epigrams, but they are reserved, as a rule, for serious subjects. This epigram demonstrates Meleager's interest in examining the psychological effects of love in a genre which usually treats love in a more superficial manner. Meleager handles the trope with considerable finesse.

1 ἐνύπνιον: "dream".

5 μνήμης πόθος: "longing for the thing remembered".

5-6 ὕπνον ἀγρευτὴν πτηνοῦ φάσματος: "sleep, hunter of the fleeting phantom".

118

The Chanticleer (*A. P.* 12. 137)

Small and threatening creatures make their appearance once again, this time in the form of a noisy rooster. The morning song is written in Meleager's elevated style.

1 τρισάλαστε: "many times accursed".

2 πλευροτυπῆ κέλαδον: "a wing-flapping [side-striking] clarion".

3 ὑπὲρ κοίτας: "arrogant about his mating" (J. Moore-Blunt). Roosters are traditionally lecherous in Greek and Roman literature (Aristotle *G.A.* 749b, *H.A.* 448b4). The rooster who mates in daylight is τρισάλαστος because the poet's time for love is almost over with the coming of dawn.

5 βαθὺν ὄρθρον: "early morning".

119

On Love's High Seas (*A. P.* 12. 157)

4 Meleager puns on the word πάμφυλος, which both means "of many races" and is also a geographical designation, "Pamphylian". The Pamphylian Sea lay along the southern coast of Turkey, extending in an arc between Lycia (on the west), Cilicia (on the east), and Pisidia (on the north). The *sinus Pamphylius* (Strabo 14. 3. 9; 6. 1) did not have a reputation for bad weather.

120

Ares' Trophies (*A. P.* 6. 163)

A dedicatory epigram of this type, emerging from a welter of amatory verse, is somewhat of a surprise. The same theme is treated in the *Anthology* by Leonidas of Tarentum (*A. P.* 9. 322) and by Antipater of Sidon (*A. P.* 9. 323); both poems are Meleager's models. For a discussion of these three epigrams, see A. Wifstrand, *Studien zur Griechischen Anthologie* (Lund 1926) 40-41.

Meleager

The epigram incorporates a great deal of Homeric and pseudo-Homeric vocabulary appropriate to the theme. The epigram is spoken by Ares.

1 μοι: that is, "for me [Ares]".

2 Ἐνυαλίου: "Ares". While the epithet Enyalius ("warlike") appears frequently in the *Iliad* to describe Ares, in later times Enyalius and Ares were conceived as two distinct gods. The name appears to be derived from Enyo, a war goddess who corresponds to the Roman Bellona.

3 περιαγέες: "broken".

4 ἄρηρε: A form of ἀραρίσκω.

121

Heraclitus (*A. P.* 7. 79)

While famous figures of other days are a common topic for poets, this epigram is Meleager's only contribution to the "genre". The only other vivid dialogue found in this poet's *oeuvre* (Selection 130) is of uncertain authorship. See M. L. West, "An Epigram on Heraclitus," *CR* 17 (1967) 127-28, and H. Lloyd-Jones, "Again Meleager's Epigram on Heraclitus," *CR* 18 (1967) 21.

See Diogenes Laertius 9. 1 for the traditional details of Heraclitus' life.

2 φαμί...σοφίας: "Indeed, but one's services to one's country are more important than one's *sophia* [i.e. one's speculative discoveries]".

3 λάξ: Although this word means "under foot", here it clearly means "rudely". **τοκεῶνας**: "fathers", not "my parents". Heraclitus says (Diels-Kranz, *Frag. der Vorsokratiker* B 20): "After being born, men wish to live and have deaths; they leave children behind to be their deaths." The two lines then read, "...for you even (treated) fathers rudely". And Heraclitus replies, "See here, sir, I barked at foolish men."

4-5 Οὐκ ἀπ' ἐμεῦ: "Won't you get away from me?"

5-6 Μὴ...πάτρας: "Not so rough, since you may soon hear something rougher from your fatherland."

6 Σὺ δ' ἐξ Ἐφέσου: "And you, just get out of Ephesus."

122

Antipater's Epitaph (*A. P.* 7. 428)

The poet imagines that he is standing before the tombstone of

98

Antipater of Sidon. See note to Selection 1, line 42, for the particulars of Antipater's career.

The imaginary tombstone bears the name ANTIPATER in addition to several symbols which serve to identify the poet. The technique is used elsewhere by Meleager in his own "epitaph" (Selection 5), and is used several times by Antipater himself (*A. P.* 7. 303, 424, and 425). The example here is the longest and most elaborate of all. First the symbols are described; next a series of possibilities is advanced and rejected; finally the symbols are cogently explained in the context of Antipater's reputation, origin, accomplishments, and demise.

1 σύνθημα τί σοι γοργωπὸς ἐλέκτωρ: "What token is that bright-eyed cock which...?"

2 καλλαΐνᾳ: "blue-green".

5-6 The first possibility: a king.

7-8 The second suggestion: a poor man.   **λιτός**: "plain".

9-10 The third suggestion: the winner of a foot race.

11 οὐ...τᾷδε: "But I do not hit the mark with that".   **ταχὺς ἀνήρ**: "a runner".

15 περὶ Κύπριν: See Selection 118, line 3.

16 ποικίλος: "versatile".

17 The scepter is the symbol of eloquence.

17-18 The crux of the riddle lies in these lines, one perhaps easy for the ancients to identify, but difficult for moderns. It depends on the identification of the "brand" of wine with which Antipater was intoxicated and the meaning of the same word in a game of dice. It is Chian wine, a sweet white (λευκός). But the expression also suggests a bad throw of the dice. We know this from Leonidas of Tarentum (*A. P.* 7. 422. 1-4), who says:

Τί στοχασώμεθά σου, Πεισίστρατε, χῖον ὁρῶντες
  γλυπτὸν ὑπὲρ τύμβου κείμενον ἀστράγαλον;
ἦ ῥά γε μὴ ὅτι Χῖος; ἔοικε γάρ· ἦ ῥ᾽ ὅτι παίκτας
  ἦσθά τις, οὐ λίην δ᾽, ὦ 'γαθέ, πλειστοβόλος;

The throw was represented by one of the two narrower sides of the ἀστράγαλος and was counted as "one". The opposite side was counted as "six", the highest throw. Because of its proximity to Leonidas' epigram, Gow and Page suggest that the poem was written expressly for inclusion in the *Garland* and not intended for any other context.

123

Clearista's Bridal Night (*A. P.* 7. 182)

The death of a bride on her wedding night is not an uncommon topic in the *Anthology* (see Antipater of Sidon, *A. P.* 7. 711; Callimachus, *A. P.* 7. 517; and Erinna, *A. P.* 7. 712). Although not very original, the writing reflects Meleager's customary stylishness.

1 ἐπινυμφίδιον: "as a bridal gift".

3 δικλίσιν: The double folding door of the house. ἄχευν: Imperfect of ἠχέω.

4 ἐπλαταγεῦντο: "echoed to the clapping of hands".

5 Ὑμέναιος: "the bridal song".

6 μεθαρμόσατο: "was altered to".

124

Aesigines (*A. P.* 7. 461)

This brief epigram in memory of a departed acquaintance reiterates the oft-repeated theme of *sit tibi terra levis*.

125

The Death of Charixenus (*A. P.* 7. 468)

1-2 Proper adornment of the deceased was of prime concern. For the χλαμύς, see Selection 83, note to line 1. Corpses were customarily dressed in white for interment. See Antipater of Sidon (*A. P.* 7. 467).

7 κακοπάρθενε: "cursed maid".

8 "Barren of offspring, you have spat affection to the wind" (Page), an arresting phrase.

9 πάρα = πάρεστι: "it remains for…".

10 οἶς δ' ἀγνὼς πευθομένοις ἐλεεῖν: "and for those to whom you are unknown to pity when they learn of you".

126

The Death of Daphnis (*A. P.* 7. 535)

The epigram appears to be a dedication for a work of art, and is the only poem of Meleager with mythological material in the foreground. Other treatments of such matter relegate the mythology to the background, using it, as a rule, in a personal amatory context; see, for example, the Ganymede series, Selections 84 and 101. Daphnis appears also in Selection 88.

3 τί ποθεινὸν: "delightful".
6 τὰ πάροιθ'…φίλα: "former lovers".

127

Bacchus' Birth (*A. P.* 9. 331)
Like Selection 113, this epigram mixes erotic and sympotic themes. It introduces a double conceit: that of the opposition of water and wine, and of the contrast between fire and water. Bacchus was born at the very moment his mother Semele was consumed by a bolt of lightning.

4 δέξῃ: Future middle, second person singular.

128

On a Statue of Niobe (*A. Pl.* 134)
This amazing literary exercise is to all intents and purposes ecphrastic and inspired by a painting. It is presented as a messenger speech in a tragic drama. The diction is highly emotional while at the same time displaying Meleager's clarity. Compare Theodoridas (*A. Pl.* 132).

1 ἄτας: A genitive singular.

2 λαλιάν: The word is somewhat surprising in this context, since it most often connotes "prattle". Here it appears to mean a "tale" or a "narrative".

5 The pathos is sustained by a summary dismissal of Niobe's sons in one of those classically simply phrases οὔ σοι παῖδες ἔτ' εἰσίν, and emphasis is focused on the death agonies of Niobe's daughters.

6 "Alas, the tide of blood is full for your daughters".

9 ἄλλα: "another one". **ἀντωπὸν**: "flying at her".

12 σαρκοτακὴς: "with her flesh wasting away".

The narrative conveys the central tragedy of Tantalus' daughter's boast. It was a catastrophe she brought on herself, when in an insolent mood she boasted that her seven sons and seven daughters were superior to Artemis and Apollo. Leto took offense and sent her famous pair of children to wreak vengeance on so boastful a mortal by killing all fourteen of her children. Tradition tells us that Niobe turned to stone, and Pausanias (1. 21. 3) claims to have witnessed her granite existence extended into historical times, declaring he saw an immense relief of her (probably referable to Hittite art) on Mt. Sipylus in Lydia.

Meleager

129

The Valedictory (*A. P.* 12. 257)

This is assumed to be the final poem in Meleager's *Garland* and is called in the jargon of literary criticism a σφραγίς or "seal", in which the poet usually identifies himself as the author of the collection and appends whatever additional information he deems pertinent. The poem is a whimsical conclusion to a collection of epigrams which, although containing a number of poems on serious subjects, was designed to titillate and amuse. Some have doubted the authenticity of this little Alexandrian end note, but the style appears to be very much that of our poet.

1 καμπτῆρα: A racing term, "the final turn". **κορωνίς**: "the flourish of a pen". The κορωνίς is a common feature of manuscripts, placed at the end of a book, or chapter, or scene of a play.

2 Mention of σελίσιν betrays the common format of papyrus rolls, "columns".

4 βύβλῳ τᾷδ': A feminine noun indicating the inner surface of the papyrus and, in later times a "book".

6 μουσοπόλον: "serving the Muses".

7 οὖλα: "twisted".

8 σύνθρονος: "ensconced". **τέρμασιν εὐμαθίας**: "in the last lines of a learned work".

130

Philaulus' Epitaph (*A. P.* 7. 470)

This epigram is found in a sequence in the *Greek Anthology* dealing with self-inflicted deaths. There is some doubt as to the authorship, some critics claiming that it was written by Antipater of Sidon. The deceased is presented with a sufficiency of detail and without any conceits, leading one to believe—whoever the author was—that Philaulus might actually have existed.

1 Εἶπον: An aorist imperative. **τίνος ἐσσί**: "whose son you are."

2 εὔχεαι: "did you boast". In the *Planudean Anthology* the gap is filled with the words ἔμεν; Θριασεύς. The validity of the conjecture ἔμεν works against Meleagrian authorship, since ἔμεν is not found elsewhere in the poet's writings. On the other hand it is unlikely that Planudes would arbitrarily have introduced a reference to the obscure deme of Thria.

3 στέργων: "being glad to have (it)".

6 Κείων: Tradition tells us that Ceans who reached the age of 60 were required to drink hemlock, thus relieving the island of its excessive population (Strabo 10. 5. 6; Plutarch, *Moralia* 249D). Philaulus seems to have committed suicide in keeping with his philosophical beliefs.

131
There Is No Escape (*A. Pl.* 213)

This is another epigram whose authorship is in doubt. It is ascribed as well to Strato, a second century A.D. Sardian epigrammatist.

2 ἀκροβολεῖς: "sharp-pointed".

4 We must presume that Hades' love affair was with Persephone, since he is not reported to have been enamored of anyone else.

132
Archilochus' Scorn (*A. P.* 7. 352)

The fate of the daughters of Lycambes is one of the better known literary fictions of antiquity. Archilochus, the seventh century B.C. Parian poet, reportedly became enamored of Neobule, daughter of Lycambes; but the father broke off the engagement. We are told that Archilochus' subsequent verses, filled with venomous accusations and threats, finally drove father and all of his daughters to suicide. The same tale is told of Hipponax. See Gaetulicus' literary epitaph for Archilochus (*A. P.* 7. 71).

1-2 The oaths sworn here are uncommon and, as far as we can see, inappropriate. Oaths were sealed by a handclasp, as Δεξιτερὴν χέρα implies. If an oath were to be sworn, it would be more appropriate that it be sworn by a maiden goddess, since the daughters of Lycambes continued to protest their innocence. Persephone was the consort of Hades, and so no longer enjoyed that status. ἀρρήτου: "whose name should not be mentioned".

3 καὶ: "even though".

5 καλὴν φάτιν: "beautiful language", presumably his beautiful style, since his language was notoriously on the abusive side.

7 Πιερίδες: A patronymic of the Muses, whose father was Pierus, king of Emathia.

SOURCE OF THE EPIGRAMS

Anthologia Palatina			
Book 4.	1	Selection	1
Book 5.	8		69
	24		41
	57		14
	96		59
	136		42
	137		43
	139		29
	140		30
	141		44
	143		45
	144		31
	147		46
	148		47
	149		32
	151		33
	152		34
	154		63
	155		48
	156		25
	157		49
	160		26
	163		50
	165		51
	166		52
	171		35
	172		27
	173		28
	174		36
	175		70
	176		6
	177		37
	178		38
	179		7
	180		8
	182		71
	184		72
	187		58
	190		64
	191		73
	192		57
	195		39
	196		40
	197		23
	198		24
	204		60
	208		9
	212		10
	214		53
	215		54
Book 6.	162		11
	163		120
Book 7.	79		121
	182		123
	195		12
	196		13
	207		65
	352		132
	417		2
	418		3
	419		4
	421		5
	428		122
	461		124
	468		125
	470		130
	476		56
	535		126
Book 9.	16		74
	331		127

Source of the Epigrams

Book 12.	Selection		
23	99	122	85
33	90	125	117
41	94	126	87
47	15	127	79
48	16	128	88
49	113	132	21, 22
52	81	133	84
53	66	137	118
54	82	141	96
56	110	144	106
57	111	147	55
59	100	154	107
60	95	157	119
63	91	158	93
65	101	159	108
68	112	164	80
70	102	165	98
72	92	167	109
74	97	256	78
76	89	257	129
78	83		
80	17	*Anthologia*	
81	86	*Planudea*	
82	67	134	128
83	68	213	131
84	114		
85	115		
86	18		
92	116		
94	76		
95	77		
101	103		
106	104		
109	61		
110	105		
113	62		
114	75		
117	19		
119	20		

INDEX OF PROPER NAMES

Meleager

Charidamus: 112. 1.

Charites (poems by Meleager): 2. 4; 3. 6; 5. 14.

Charites (*The Graces*): 30. 4; 32. 2, 4; 39. 1; 40. 2; 43. 2; 47. 2; 74. 1; 77. 2; 85. 1.

Charixenus: 125. 1.

Chronos: 5. 5.

Clearista: 123. 1.

Cleobulus: 80. 3; 97. 1; 98. 1.

Cleon: 72. 5.

Cos: 3. 3; 4. 6; 66. 3.

Cypris: 6. 6; 7. 1; 11. 2; 18. 1, 4; 21. 1; 39. 5; 40. 2; 43. 1; 60. 2; 63. 1; 68. 3; 73. 7; 78. 1, 12; 80. 4; 82. 1; 96. 1; 98. 2; 107. 3; 109. 4; 110. 2; 114. 8; 116. 2; 119. 1; 122. 15.

Damagetus: 1. 21.

Damis: 92. 2, 5.

Daphnis: 88. 1, 5; 126. 3, 4.

Demo: 23. 2; (Demarion: 24. 2); 26. 1; 27. 2; 28. 2.

Diocles: 1. 3; 129. 5.

Diodorus: 61. 1; 76. 1; 77. 3; 78. 3; 91. 3.

Dion: 76. 2; 77. 5; 78. 6; 88. 6.

Dionyius: 86. 5.

Diophantus: 87. 5.

Dioscorides: 1. 24.

Diotimus: 1. 27.

Dorcas: 58. 1; 71. 1, 2, 3, 4, 7.

Dorothea: 24. 4.

Dorotheus: 77. 4.

Endymion: 51. 6.

Enualius: 120. 2.

Eos: 75. 1.

Ephesus: 121. 6.

Erinna: 1. 12.

Eros: 1. 10; 4. 3; 5. 3, 13; 6. 1, 2; 7. 1; 8. 1; 10. 1; 13. 7; 14. 2; 15. 2; 17. 1, 6; 18. 2; 19. 3, 6; 20. 3; 21. 4; 22. 3; 23. 5; 24. 6; 26. 4; 30. 2; 37. 1; 39. 6; 40. 1; 44. 1; 48. 2; 49. 1; 50. 4; 53. 1; 54. 1, 6; 55. 2; 61. 3; 62. 1; 64. 1; 67. 1; 68. 1; 78. 2; 79. 3; 82. 1, 4; 83. 1, 4; 87. 2: 89. 1, 4; 92. 5; 93. 2; 97. 4; 99. 3; 100. 1; 103. 6; 105. 2; 107. 4; 109. 2; 110. 1, 3, 8; 111. 4, 8; 114. 3; 115. 4, 9; 116. 8; 117. 3; 119. 1; 131. 3.

Erotes: 9. 1; 10. 5; 29. 3; 98. 3.

Eucrates: 2. 3; 3.5; 4.3.

Eucratides: 130. 2.

Eudemus: 77. 8.

Euphemus: 1. 20.

Euphorion: 1. 23.

Gadara: 2. 2; 3. 1; 4.5.

Galene: 25. 1.

Ganymede: 84. 3; 101. 1.

Ge: 56. 9; 124. 1.

Greece: 4.8.

Hades: 2. 8; 56. 2, 7; 97. 4; 123. 1; 125. 1; 130. 5; 131. 4; 132. 1.

Hedylus: 1. 45.

Hegesippus: 1. 25.

Heliodora: 24. 1; 41. 1; 42. 1; 43. 1; 44. 1; 45. 1; 46. 5; 47. 1; 48. 1;
     49. 1; 50. 1; 51. 3; 52. 1; 53. 1; 54. 1; 55. 3; 56. 1.

Hellespont: 66. 1.

Hephaestus: 8. 4, 7.

Heraclitus (*eromenos*): 76. 1; 78. 5; 90. 1; 91. 1; 92. 3.

Heraclitus (*philosophos*): 121. 1.

Hermadorus: 1. 44.

Hermes: 1. 44.

Hesperus: 27. 3; 75. 2.

Himerus: 5. 4; 82. 2.

Horai: 74. 1.

Hyacinthus: 88. 4, 5.

Hymenaeus: 123. 5.

Hypnos: 36. 3.

Ilias: 23. 3.

Leonidas of Tarentum: 1. 15.

Leto (in reference to Artemis): 5. 9; (in reference to Apollo):
     44. 2.

Logos: 30. 1.

Lycaenis: 58. 1.

Melanippides: 1. 7.

Meleager (*poêta*): 1. 3; 2. 3; 3. 5; 4. 3; 11. 1; 56. 5; 73.7; 129. 5.

Meleager (*kunagos*): 5. 11.

Menecrates: 1. 28.

Menippus: 2. 4; 3. 6.

Meropes: 3. 4; 4. 6; 110. 7.

Mnasalcus: 1. 16.

Moero: 1. 5.

Moira: 125. 7.

Muse(s): 1. 1, 23, 33, 55, 58; 2. 3; 3. 5; 4. 4; 5. 13; 12. 2; 30. 1; 122. 16; 132. 7.

Myiscus: 76. 5; 78. 9; 99. 3; 100.1; 101. 3; 102. 1; 103. 1; 104. 2; 105. 3; 106. 3; 107. 1; 108. 1; 109. 1.

Nemesis: 90. 4; 96. 6.

Nicaenetus: 1. 29.

Nicias: 1. 20.

Niobe: 128. 1.

Nossis: 1. 10.

Notus: 81. 1.

Nymphs: 13. 5; 127. 1, 3.

Nyx: 51. 1, 2; 52. 1; 69. 1; 73. 2.

Oeneus: 5. 11.

Olympus: 85. 5; 103. 6; 112. 5.

Ouliades: 76. 2; 77. 6; 78. 8.

Pamphilus: 1. 17.

Pan: 13. 6; 29. 1, 2; 88. 2; 126. 2, 6.

Pancrates: 1. 18.

Paros: 110. 1.

Parthenis: 1. 32.

Peitho: 31. 4; 39. 6; 43. 1; 77. 2.

Persephone: 132. 2.

Perses: 1. 26.

Phaedimus: 1. 52.

Phaennus: 1. 29.

Phanias: 1. 54.

Phanion: 65. 4; 66. 4; 67. 6.

Philaulus: 130. 1.

Philo: 77. 7.

Philocles: 76. 3; 77. 1.

Phoebus: 88. 3; 128. 3.

Phoenicia: 4. 7.

Phoenicians: 1. 42; 122. 14.

Pierides: 132. 7.

Plato: 1. 47.

Polyclitus: 1. 40.

Polystratus: 1. 41.

Polyxenides: 90. 3.

Posidippus: 1. 45.

Pothoi (or Pothos): 7. 5; 10. 2; 30. 3; 53. 3; 68. 3; 74. 2; 77. 1; 82. 3; 88. 6; 89. 2; 91. 6; 93. 1; 103. 1; 105. 3; 109. 3; 110. 6; 119. 3.

Praxiteles (*lithourgos*): 110. 2; 111. 1.

Praxiteles (*eromenos*): 110. 4.

Ptolemy II Philadelphus: 3. 3.

Rhianus: 1. 11.

Rhodes: 81. 6.

Rome: 77. 10.

Samius: 1. 14.

Sappho: 1. 6.

Scylla: 64. 4.

Scythians: 7. 2; 131. 2.

Selene: 73. 1.

"Sicelides": 1. 46.

Simias: 1. 30.

"Simonides": 1. 8.

Sophrosyne: 99. 4.

Sopolis: 98. 2.

Syracuse: 57. 2.

Syria: 1. 43; 2. 5; 4. 7.

Tantalus (referring to Niobe): 128. 1.

Thalassa: 8. 5.

Theocles: 93. 1.

Theodoridas: 1. 53.

Theron: 77. 7; 78. 7; 94. 1; 95. 1; 96. 2, 3.

Timarion: 59. 1; 60. 1; 61. 2; 62. 2.

Timo: 23. 1; 24. 1.

Tryphera: 63. 2; 64. 4.

Tymnes: 1. 19.

Tyre: 2. 1; 3. 2; 4. 5; 78. 11; 100. 1; 122. 14.

Zenophila: 29. 2; 30. 3; 31. 4; 32. 1; 33. 3; 34. 2; 35. 2; 36. 1; 37. 10; 38. 10; 39. 2; 40. 1.

Zeus: 1. 24; 3. 3; 17. 3; 19. 6; 27. 5; 36. 3; 66. 7; 84. 3; 85. 6; 91. 2; 96. 4; 101. 1; 102. 1, 6; 103. 6; 112. 1, 9.

Zoilus: 89. 4.

VOCABULARY

A

ἀβαρής, -ές   adj.   not burdensome or heavy

ἁβροκόμης, -ου   m.   with luxuriant hair

ἁβροπέδιλος, -ον   adj.   soft-sandalled

ἁβρός, -ά, -όν   adj.   graceful, pretty, delicate

ἄγαλμα, -ατος   n.   a statue in honor of a god, the image of a god

ἀγγελία, -ας   f.   a message, news

ἄγγελος, -ου   m.   a messenger; a message

ἀγγέλλω, -ελῶ, ἤγγειλα, ἤγγελον (2 Aor.)   to bear a message, proclaim

ἀγέομαι (ἡγέομαι), -ήσομαι   to lead, guide

ἀγκαλίζομαι, -ίσομαι   to take up in the arms, lift up (ἠγκαλίσασθε 2nd Pl. Aor. Indic. Mid.)

ἀγκάς   adv.   into or in the arms

ἀγλαΐζω, -ισω   to make splendid, adorn

ἀγνώς, -ῶτος   m. and f.   being unknown; obscurity

ἀγρευτής, -οῦ   m.   a hunter

ἀγρεύω, -εύσω, ἠγρεύθην (Aor. Pass.)   to hunt, catch

ἄγρη, -ης   f.   a hunting; the prey

ἄγριος, -ία, -ιον   adj.   living in the fields, living wild, savage

ἀγρόνομος, -ον   adj.   rural, wild

ἄγρυπνος, -ον   adj.   sleepless, keeping awake

ἄγω, ἄξω, ἤγαγον (ἄγαγον)   to lead; bring

ἀδαής, -ές   adj.   ignorant, unpracticed

ἀδύλογος, -ον   adj.   sweet-voiced

ἀδύπνοος, -ον = ἡδύπνοος

ἁδύς, -έα, -ύ = ἡδύς

ἀεί   adv.   always, ever

ἀείδω, ἀείσομαι   to sing

ἀειθαλής, -ές   adj.   ever-green, ever-blooming

ἀείλαλος, -ον   adj.   always talking

ἀείμνηστος, -η, -ον   adj.   everlasting, ever-memorable

ἀείρω, ἀρῶ   to lift up; to win, take (Mid.); arise (Pass.)

ἀήρ, ἀέρος   f.   air

ἀθαμβής, -ές   adj.   fearless

ἀθλοφόρος, -ον   adj.   victorious

113

ἄθρεπτος, -ον   adj.   un-nurtured, unable to be nursed

ἀθρέω, -ήσω   to gaze, see

ἀθροίζω, -οίσω   to gather together, collect

αἰάζω   to cry, to wail

αἰαί   interj.   oh! (exclam. of astonishment)

αἰγανέη, -ης   f.   a hunting spear, javelin

αἰγιβάτης, -ου   m.   goat-mounting

αἰδέομαι, -έσομαι, ἠδέσθην (Aor. Pass.)   to be ashamed; to be rec-
    onciled, pardon (Pass.)

Ἀΐδης, -αο and -εω   m.   Hades, god of the underworld

ᾄδω = ἀείδω

αἰγοβάτης, -ου   m. = αἰγιβάτης

αἰεί, αἰέν = ἀεί

αἰθήρ, -έρος   m. and f.   sky, heaven

αἰθίοψ, -οπος   m.   one with a burnt face; as adj.: sunburned

αἴθω   to light up, kindle

αἰκίζω, αἰκίσομαι   to torment, outrage

αἷμα, αἵματος   n.   blood

αἱματόφυρτος, -ον   adj.   blood-stained

αἰπολικός, -ή, -όν   adj.   belonging to goatherds

αἰπόλιον, -ου   n.   a herd of goats

αἱρέω, αἱρήσω, εἷλον   to take, seize, catch; to choose, prefer
    (Mid.)

αἰσχρός, -ά, -όν   adj.   causing shame or disgrace; disgraceful

αἰώρητος, -ον   adj.   hanging

ἄκανθα, -ης   f.   a thorn, thistle

ἀκίς, -ίδος   f.   a point, barb; a spear

    πόθων ἀκίδες   the stings of desire

ἀκλινής, -ές   adj.   inflexible, steadfast

ἀκμαῖος, -αία, -αῖον   adj.   in full bloom, vigorous

ἀκμή, -ῆς   f.   the highest point of anything, the bloom, prime

ἀκοίμητος, -ον   adj.   sleepless, unresting

ἀκόλαστος, -ον   adj.   undisciplined; licentious

ἀκρέμων, -ονος   m.   a bough, branch

ἄκρητος, -ον   adj.   pure, unmixed

ἀκρίς, -ίδος   f.   a locust

ἀκροβολέω   to throw from afar, sling

ἀκροθιγής, -ές   adj.   touching lightly

ἀκρονυχεῖ (ἀκρονυχί)   adv.   with the tip of the nail

ἄκρος, -α, -ον   adj.   at the end or edge, outermost

ἀκρώνυχος, -ον   adj.   having nails

   χερὸς ἀκρώνυχα   the tips of the fingers

ἀκτίς, -ίνος   f.   a ray, beam

ἄκων, ἄκουσα, ἄκον   adj.   against one's will, involuntarily

ἀλέκτωρ, -ορος   m.   a cock

ἄλιξ, -ικος = ἧλιξ

ἀλίσκομαι, ἀλώσομαι, ἥλων, ἀλώσει (2nd sg. Fut. Mid.)   to be
   taken, be conquered

ἀλλά   adv.   but

ἄλλαγμα, -ατος   n.   that which is changed, interchanged; the
   price to be paid

ἀλλάττω (ἀλάσσω), -άξω, ἤλλαγμαι (Perf. Pass.)   to change, alter

ἄλλοθι   adv.   elsewhere, in another place

ἄλλομαι, ἀλοῦμαι, ἡλάμην, ἡλόμην (2 Aor.)   to spring, leap

ἄλλος, -η, -ο   adj.   other

ἄλλοφος, -ον   adj.   without a crest

ἅλς, ἁλός   m. or f.   a lump of salt (m.); the sea (f.)

ἄλσος, -εος   n.   a grove of trees and grass

ἄλυτος, -ον   adj.   not to be loosened

ἀλύω   to wander, roam about, to be weary

ἅμα   adv.   at the same time

ἀμάρακον, -ου   n.   marjoram

ἀμάω, -ήσω   to gather together (ἀμησάμενος 1 Aor. Part.)

ἀμβροσία, -ας   f.   ambrosia

ἀμείνων, -ον   adj.   better

ἄμμα, -ατος   n.   a knot, anything tied

   ἄμμα παρθενίας   the maiden girdle

ἀμμότροφος, -ον   adj.   growing in sand

ἄμπαλιν = ἀνάπαλιν

ἀμπνέω (ἀναπνέω), -πνεύσομαι   to recover breath, revive

ἀμφήκης, -ες   adj.   two-edged, double-edged, cutting both ways,
   ambiguous

ἀμφί   prep.   with gen.: about, for the sake of, concerning;
   around
    with dat.: about, around; at, by, near, with; for
    with acc.: around, on

ἀμφιβάλλω, -αλῶ   to put round; grasp (in an embrace)

ἀμφιτίθημι   to lay or put round, to wear

115

ἀμφότερος, -έρα, -ερον   adj.   both

ἀμώμητος, -ον   blameless, unblemished

ἄν   part.; implies a condition (often unable to be translated) with Optative, Subjunctive and Indicative. Sometimes stands for ἐάν

ἀναδείκνυμι, -δείξω   to exhibit, display

ἀνάδεσμος, -ου   m.   a headband

ἀναιδής, -ές   adj.   shameless, bold

ἀναίνομαι, ἠνηνάμην (Aor.)   to refuse, reject, renounce

ἀνακράζω, -άξομαι, ἀνέκραγον   to cry out

ἀναλέγω, -λέξω   to pick up, gather up

    ἀναλέγεσθαι πνεῦμα   to collect one's breath

ἀναμίξ   adv.   mixed up, all together

ἄναξ, ἄνακτος   m.   a lord, king (applied to all the gods)

ἀνάπαλιν   adv.   back again, over again

ἀνάπτω, -ψω   to fasten onto, hang onto; to light, light up

ἀνατρέφω, ἀναθρέψω, ἀνέθρεχα, ἀνέτραφον (2 Aor.)   to restore by nourishment; to bring up, make to grow

ἀναφθέγγομαι, -γξομαι   to call out aloud or again, to answer

ἀναφλογίζω, -ίσω   to light up, rekindle

ἀναψύχω, -ψύξω   to refresh, cool

ἀνδάνω, ἀδήσω, ἔαδον (ἅδον)   to please, gratify

ἀνδροβατέω, -ήσω   to have anal intercourse

ἀνδρόω, -ώσω   to make a man of

ἀνεγείρω, -ερῶ   to wake up, rouse

ἄνειμι   to go up, mount (ἀνιών   Nom. Sg. Pres. Part.)

ἀνείρομαι   to ask, inquire

ἄνεμος, -ου   m.   wind, breeze

    ἀνέμοις ἄνθεα φυόμενα   anemones

ἀνευρίσκω, -ρήσω, ἀνεῦρον (2 Aor.)   to find out, discover

ἀνήρ, ἀνδρός   m.   a man (ἀνήρ = ὁ ἀνήρ)

ἄνθεμα, -ατος   n.   a votive offering

ἀνθέμιον, -ου   n.   a bloom

ἄνθη, -ης   f.   a blossom, bloom

ἄνθησις, -εως = ἄνθη

ἀνθοβολέω   to throw flowers at someone, to cover with flowers

ἀνθοδίαιτος, -ον   adj.   living on flowers

ἀνθολόγος, -ον   adj.   picking, gathering flowers

ἄνθος, -εος   n.   a young bud or sprout; a single flower blossom, a bloom ἀνθοφόρος, -ον   adj.   flowery, bearing flowers

ἀνθρακιή, -ῆς   f.   hot coals, a heap of coal

ἀνίημι, ἀνήσω   to let go, to let loose; to relax, slacken (ἀνείς 2 Aor. Part.)

ἀνιηρός, -ή, -όν (ἀνιαρός)   adj.   injurious, distressing

ἀνίκα = ἡνίκα

ἀνίστημι, ἀναστήσω   to raise, set up (transitive); to stand up, rise (intransitive)

ἄνταθλος, -ον   adj.   rivalling

ἀνταίρω, -αρῶ   to raise against, raise up against (ἀντᾶραι Aor. Inf.)

ἀντίος, -ία, -ίον   adj.   set against, opposite; before one, in one's presence (with gen.)

ἀντῳδός, -όν   singing in answer to, responding

ἀντωπός, -όν   adj.   facing, looking straight at

ἀνύτω (ἀνύω), ἀνύσω, ἤνυσα (ἄνυσα)   gain, accomplish; create

ἄνωθεν (ἄνωθα)   adv.   from above, above; from the beginning

ἀνωρύομαι   to howl, scream out loud

ἄξιος, -ία, -ιον   adj.   worthy

ἀοιδή, -ῆς   f.   song; legend, tale (the subject of a song)

ἀπάγω, ἀπάξω   to lead away, carry off; bring back

ἀπάλαιστρος, -ον   adj.   awkward, clumsy; not trained in sports, unsportsmanlike

ἀπαλός, -ή, -όν   adj.   tender, soft, gentle

ἀπαλόχροος, -ον   adj.   soft or fine skinned

ἀπαναίνομαι   to refuse completely, reject utterly

ἀπαστράπτω, -ψω   to flash forth

ἀπάτημα, -ατος   n.   cheating, deceit

ἀπεικονίζω, -ίσω   to express, represent, portray

ἀπειλέω, -ήσω   to threaten; boast, vow

ἀπέχθομαι   to be hated

ἄπιστος, -ον   adj.   not to be trusted, faithless

ἄπληστος, -ον   adj.   insatiate, not to be filled up

ἀπνευστί   adv.   without breathing, at one gulp

ἀπό   prep.   with gen.: from, away from, in succession to

ἀποδρέπω, -ψω   to pluck off; to gather for oneself (Mid.)

ἀποθερίζω, -ίσω, ἀπέθρισα (contr. Aor.)   to cut off, pluck

ἀπονέμω, -νεμῶ, ἀπένειμα   to assign, distribute

ἀποπέτομαι, ἀποπτήσομαι   to fly off or away

ἀπόπλους, -ου m. an outward-bound voyage or journey

ἀποπροφεύγω, ἀποπρούφυγον (2 Aor.) to flee far away from

ἀποψύχω, -ξω to faint; to breathe out

ἄπτερος, -ον adj. without wings

ἄπτω, ἄψω to fasten, fix; to touch; to kindle, light

ἄρα part. so then, perhaps, after all, too

ἆρα interogg. part. introduces a question that expects a negative answer

ἀραρίσκω to join, fit together

ἀρετή, -ῆς f. virtue, excellence

ἀρήν, ἀρνός m. and f. a lamb, a sheep

ἀρίζαλος (ἀρίζηλος), -ον adj. of persons whom all admire; glorious, well- known

ἀρκέω, -έσω to ward off; to assist, aid; to be satisfied, contented (Pass.)

ἁρμόζω, -όσω to fit together, join

ἀρνέομαι, -ήσομαι to deny, refuse

ἄροτρον, -ου n. a plough

ἄρουρα, -ας f. cornfield

ἀρουραῖος, -αία, -αῖον adj. belonging to a cornfield, rustic

ἁρπάζω, ἁρπάσω (ἁρπάξω), ἥρπασα, ἥρπακα, ἥρπασμαι, ἡρπάσθην to carry off, seize

ἁρπαστός, -ή, -όν adj. to be caught, swept away

ἄρρητος, -η, -ον adj. unspoken, not made known, secret

ἀρσενικός (ἀρρενικός), -ή, -όν adj. male

ἀρσενόπαις, -παιδος m. and f. of a boy

ἄρσην, -εν adj. masculine, manly

ἀρτεμής, -ές adj. safe and sound; as adv.: quietly, gently

ἄρτι adv. just, exactly, even now

ἀρτιβρεχής, -ές adj. just steeped, moist

ἀρτιθαλής, -ές adj. just blooming or budding

ἀρτύω, -ύσω to arrange, contrive; prepare; to dress or to season (culinary term)

ἄρχω, ἄρξω, ἦρξα, ἦρχα, ἦργμαι to begin; to lead, rule

ἄσπορος, -ον adj. not sown, untilled

'Ασσύριος, -α, -ον adj. = Σύριος

ἀστήρ, -έρος m. a star

ἀστός, -οῦ m. a citizen, a fellow citizen

ἀστράγαλος, -ου m. one of the vertebrae; dice (pl.)

ἀστράπτω, ψω   (as an impersonal) to flash with lightening

ἄστρον, -ου   n.   a star, constellation

ἄστυ, -εος (-ους)   n.   a city, town

ἀστυφέλικτος, -ον   adj.   undisturbed

ἀτάρ   conj.   but, yet, however, nevertheless

ἄτεγκτος, -ον   adj.   unsoftened; hard-hearted, merciless

ἄτη, ἄτας   f.   evil, delusion, folly

'Ατθίς, -ίδος   f.   Attica

ἀτρεκής, -ές   adj.   strict, exact, true

ἄτρωτος, -ον   adj.   invulnerable

αὐγή, -ῆς   bright light; rays, beams (pl.)

αὐδάω, -ήσω   to speak, say, call, invoke

αὖθις   adv.   back, again, in turn

ἄϋπνος, -ον   adj.   sleepless

αὐτίκα   adv.   straightway, immediately

αὐτοθελεί   adv.   voluntarily

αὐτόματος, -η, -ον   adj.   self-moving, self-acting, acting of one's
   own will

αὐτομολέω   to desert, run off

αὐτός, αὐτή, αὐτό   pron.   self (as reflex.); he, she, it (as pers.
   pron. in oblique cases); same (accompanied by article)

αὐτοφυής, -ές   adj.   natural, self-existent

αὔτως   adv.   even so, just so

αὐχήν, -ένος   m.   the neck, throat

αὐχμηρός, -ά, -όν   adj.   dry, thirsty

ἀφαρπάζω, -άξω   to snatch, clasp

ἄφθονος, -ον   adj.   free from envy, not jealous

ἀφίημι, -ήσω   to send forth, send away

ἀφύσσω, ἀφύξω, ἤφυσα   to draw (liquids); to drink (Mid.)

ἀχέω (ἠχέω)   to sound

ἀχήεις (ἠχήεις), -εσσα, -εν   adj.   sounding, ringing

ἀχθοφορέω   to bear burdens

ἀχράς, -άδος   f.   wild pear

ἄψυχος, -ον   adj.   lifeless

B

βαθμίς, -ίδος   f.   a pedestal

βαθύς, -εία, -ύ   adj.   deep, thick
   βαθὺς ὄρθρος   early dawn
βαίνω, βήσω, ἔβησα, ἔβην (2 Aor.)   to make to go, put in motion; 2
   Aor. is intransitive: go, reach
βαιός, -ά, -όν   adj.   little, insignificant, few
βάλλω, βαλῶ, ἔβαλον, βέβληκα, βέβλημαι, ἐβλήθην   to throw, cast
βαρέω, βεβάρημαι (Perf. Mid.)   to weigh down
βαρύμοχθος, -ον   adj.   suffering heavily, painfully afflicted
βαρυπενθής, -ές   adj.   mourning heavily, causing deep grief
βαρύς, -εῖα, -ύ   adj.   heavy, burdensome, weighty
βαρύφρων, -ον   adj.   indignant
βασιλεῦς, -έως   m.   a king, lord, prince
βαστακτός, -ή, -όν   adj.   to be borne
βέλος, -εος   n.   an arrow, dart, shaft
βίαιος, -α, -ον   adj.   forcible, violent; forced
βίος, -ου   m.   life
βίοτος, -ου   m.   manner or way of life
βλαισός, -ή, -όν   adj.   twisted; a plane-tree bending every way
βλαστάνω, βλαστήσω, ἔβλαστον   to grow, burst forth, spring
   (from)
βλέμμα, -ατος   n.   a glance
βλέπω, -ψω, ἐβλέφθην (Aor. Pass.)   to look, see
βλέφαρον, -ου   n.   the eyelids (used mostly in plural)
βλύζω (βλύω), βλύσω   to gush forth, pour out
βλωθρός, -ά, -όν   adj.   shooting up, tall-growing
βοάω, βοήσω   to shout, thunder, roar
βοηθέω, -ήσω   to assist, come to the rescue
βορέας, -ου   m.   the North wind
βόσκω, βοσκήσω   to feed, nourish
βότρυς, -υος   m.   cluster, bunch of grapes
βούλομαι, βουλήσομαι   to will, be willing; to prefer
βοῦς, βοός   m. and f.   a cow, ox
βοῶπις, -ιδος   f.   ox-eyed, having large round eyes
βραβεύω   to direct, decide
βραδύς, -εῖα, -ύ   slow, heavy
βραχύς, -εῖα, -ύ   adj.   small, short, little
βρέχω, -ξω   to wet, moisten; to be drenched (Pass.)
βρόμιος, -α, -ον   adj.   sounding, noisy
βρότεος, -έη, -εον   adj.   mortal, human

βροτολοιγός, -ον adj.   a plague to man, man-slaying
βύβλος, -ου f.   the Egyptian papyrus
βῶλος, -ου f.   ground, soil

Γ

γᾶ = γῆ
γαῖα, -ης f. = γῆ
γαλήνη, -ης f.   calm, stillness of wind and wave
γαμέτις, -ιδος f.   a wife
γαμήλιος, -ον adj.   belonging to a marriage; bridal
γάμος, -ου m.   a wedding, marriage
γανόω, -ώσω   to make bright, to polish
γάρ conj.   for; since, as
γαστήρ, -έρος f.   the belly
γαῦρος, -ον adj.   haughty
γε part.   emphasizes words which it follows: at least, surely, at
    any rate (not always translated)
γείνομαι   to be born
γειτονέω (γειτνιάω)   to be a neighbor, to border on
γείτων, -ονος m. and f.   a neighbor
γελάω, γελάσομαι   to laugh, smile
γελόω = γελάω
γέλως, -ωτος m. laughter, laughing (γέλωτα   acc.)
γεμίζω, -ίσω   to fill; be full (Pass.)
γενέτης, -ου m.   a begetter, father
γεννάω, -ήσω, ἐφεννήθην (Aor. Pass.)   to beget, generate
γέρας, -αος n.   a gift of honor, attribute
γεύομαι, γεύσομαι   to taste
γῆ (γᾶ), γῆς f.   earth
γηθέω, -ήσω, γέγηθα   to be delighted, rejoice
γῆρας, -αος (-ως) n.   advanced age, old age
γηροτροφέω   to tend to or feed old people
γηρύω, -ύσω   to speak, sing
γήτειον, -ου n.   a leek
γίγνομαι, γενήσομαι, ἐγενόμην, γέγονα, γεγένημαι   to become,
    be; come to; arise
γιγνώσκω, γνώσομαι, ἔγνων, ἔγνωκα, ἔγνωσμαι, ἐγνώσθην   to
    know, perceive, learn (γνῶθι 2nd sg. 2 Aor. Imperat. Act.)

γλαυκός, -ή, -όν   adj.   pale green, blue-green
γλαφυρός, -ά, -όν   adj.   hollow
γλουτός, -οῦ   m.   the rump, rear
γλυκερόχρως, -ωτος   m. and f.   with sweet, fair skin
γλυκύδακρυς, -υ   adj.   causing tears of joy
γλυκύμηλον, -ου   n.   a sweet-apple, summer apple
γλυκυμυθέω   to speak sweetly
γλυκύμυθος   adj.   sweet-speaking
γλυκύπαις, -αιδος   m. and f.   having beautiful offspring
γλυκυπάρθενος, -ου   f.   a sweet maiden
γλυκύπικρος, -ον   adj.   bittersweet
γλυκύς, -εῖα, -ύ   adj.   sweet
γνωστός, -ή, -όν   adj.   known, well known
γοερός, -ά, -όν   adj.   mournful
γονεύς, -έως   m.   a father; parents (pl.)
γονή, -ῆς   f.   offspring; child-birth
γόνος, -ου   m.   a child, offspring
γονύ, -ατος   n.   the knee
γοργωπός, -όν   adj.   fierce-eyed
γουνόομαι (γουνάζομαι), -σομαι   to entreat, supplicate
γράμμα, -ατος   n.   a letter
γραπτός, -ή, -όν   adj.   written, engraved
γραῦς, γραός   f.   old woman
γράφω, -ψω   to write, draw, inscribe, describe
γυῖον, -ου   n.   a limb
γυμνός, -ή, -όν   adj.   naked
γυναικεῖος, -εία, -εῖον   adj.   feminine, belonging to women
γυναικομανής, -ές   adj.   mad for women
γυνή, γυναικός   f. a woman (γύναι voc.)

Δ

δᾳδουχέω   to hold torches
δαίμων, -ονος   m. and f.   god, goddess, deity (demon)
δαίς, δαιτός   f.   a feast, banquet
δάκρυ, -υος   n.   a teardrop
δακρυχαρής, -ές   adj.   joying in tears, welcoming tears
δακρυχέων, -ουσα   shedding tears

δακρύω, -ύσω, δεδάκρυμαι (Perf. Pass.) to weep, shed tears; to be
 tearful (Pass.)

δαλός, -οῦ m. a burnt-out torch

δαμάω, δαμάσω, ἐδάμασα, ἔδαμον (2 Aor.) to overpower; to tame

δασύτρωγλος, -ον adj. with a rough or hairy posterior

δάφνη, -ης f. the bay tree

δέ part. and, but, moreover; on the other hand (in answer to
 μέν)

δεῖγμα, -ατος n. a sample, example

δείκνυμι, δείξω, ἔδειξα, δέδειγμαι (Perf. Pass.) to show, point
 out

δεινός, -ή, -όν adj. clever, powerful; terrible

δέλτος, -ου f. a writing tablet

δελφίς, -ῖνος m. the dolphin

δέμνιον, -ου n. a couch, bed

δενδρώδης, -ες adj. tree-like
  δενδρώδεις Νύμφαι wood nymphs

δεξιτερός, -ά, -όν adj. right

δέρκομαι, ἔδρακον (2 Aor.), δέδορκα (Perf. with Pres. signif.) to
 look, see; to gleam (δεδορκός neuter Perf. Part. Act.: eye,
 sight)

δέρμα, -ατος n. the skin, hide of a beast

δέρρις, -εως f. a leather covering; a screen of hide

δέσμιος, -ον adj. binding; bound, captive

δεσμός, -οῦ m. a bond, fetter

δέσποινα, -ης f. a princess, queen; a mistress

δεύτερος, -α, -ον adj. the second

δέχομαι, δέξομαι to take; accept, receive

δέω, δήσω, ἔδησα, δέδεκα to bind, tie

δή adv. accordingly, surely, indeed

διά prep. with gen.: through, at a distance of, during, by
  with acc.: through (motion), on account of, during

διακνίζω to tear to pieces, tear or pull off

διαστείχω to go straight forward; to go through or across

διατρέφω, -θρέψω to support, sustain continually, rear

διδάσκω, διδάξω, ἐδίδαξα, δεδίδαχα, δεδίδαγμαι to teach; to learn
  (Mid. and Pass.)

δίδωμι, δώσω, ἔδωκα (δῶκα), ἔδων (2 Aor.) to give, present (δοίη
 3rd sg. 2 Aor. Opt. Act.; δούς 2 Aor. Part.)

Meleager

δικλίς, -ίδος f.   double-folding (usually of doors)
Διός   gen. sg. from obs. Δίς   of Zeus
διπλοῦς, -ῆ, -οῦν   adj.   twofold, double
διπτέρυγος, -ον   adj.   with two wings
δισσός, -ή, -όν   adj.   twofold, double
δίυγρος, -ον   adj.   moistened; melting
διφυής, -ές   adj.   double, twofold; pair (substantive)
δίψα, -ης   f.   thirst
διψάω, διψήσω   to thirst
δοκέω, δόξω, ἔδοξα   to think, expect; to seem, appear (intransitive)
δορά, -ᾶς   f.   a skin, hide of a beast
δρακόντειος, -α, -ον   adj.   of a dragon or snake
δραπέτις, -ιδος   f.   a runaway, truant
δράω, δράσω, ἔδρασα   to do, accomplish, fulfill
δρέπω, -ψω   to break off; to pluck off for one's self, gather (Mid.)
δρόμος, -ου   m.   a course, race
δροσερός, -ά, -όν   adj.   full of dew, watery
δύναμαι, δυνήσομαι   to be able, capable
δύναμις, -εως   f.   strength, power, influence
δυσάμμορος, -ον   adj.   most miserable, luckless
δυσδάκρυτος, -ον   adj.   much weeping
δυσέραστος, -ον   adj.   unhappy in love, enemy of lovers
δύσερως, -ωτος   m. and f.   passionately loving, love-sick
δύσμαχος, -ον   adj.   hard to fight with; unconquerable; irresistible
δυσνίκητος, -ον   adj.   hard to conquer
δύσοιστος, -ον   adj.   hard to bear
δύστανος (δύστηνος), -ον   adj.   unhappy
δύσφρων, -ον   adj.   sorrowful; hostile
δύω (δύνω), δύσω, ἔδυσα, ἔδυν (2 Aor.)   to put on; enter, sink (intrans.)
δωρέομαι   to give, present
δωροδότης, -ου   m.   a giver of presents
δῶρον, -ου   n.   a gift

E

ἔαρ, ἔαρος   n.   spring

ἐαρινός, -ή, -όν   adj.   of or belonging to spring
ἐάω, ἐάσω, εἴασα   to let happen, suffer, allow
ἐγγελάω, -άσομαι   to laugh at, mock
ἐγγύθεν   adv.   near
ἐγείρω, ἐγερῶ, ἤγειρα, ἐγήγερκα   to awaken, rouse (ἔγρεο 2nd sg.
    2 Aor. Imperat. Mid.)
ἐγκρούω   to strike
ἔγκυον (ἐν, κύω)   adj.   heavy, laden, bursting with
ἐγχέω, ἐγχεῶ (ἐγχεύσω), ἐνέχεα   to fill the cup
ἐγώ; ἡμεῖς (pl.)   pers. pron.   I, me; we, us (pl.)
ἐθέλω, ἐθελήσω   to will, be willing; desire, wish
εἰ   conj.   if; whether
εἷα   interj.   up! come on!
εἰαρινός, -η, -ον = ἐαρινός
εἶδος, -εος   n.   form, shape; image
εἴδω (ἴδω), εἶδον (ἴδον) (Aor.)   to see (obsol. in Pres. Act., which
    is supplied by ὁράω) (ἰδέ Aor. Imperat. Act.; ἰδοῦ Aor. Imperat.
    Mid.)
εἴδωλον, -ου   n.   a shape, image
εἴθε   interj.   I wish, would that; with Opt.: expresses a desire for
    things possible but not likely
εἰκασία, -ας   f.   an image, relic
εἴκελος, -η, -ον   adj.   like, resembling
εἰκόσορος, -ον   adj.   with twenty oars
εἰκών, -όνος   f.   a figure, image; statue
εἰμί, ἔσομαι, ἦν (Imperf.)   to be
εἰν = ἐν
εἰνόδιος, -α (-η), -ον   adj.   in or on the road
εἶπον (Aor.)   to say, speak
εἴργω (ἔργω), ἔρξω   to confine; hinder, prevent
εἰρεσία, -ας   f.   a rowing; crew of rowers
εἴρω, ἐρῶ, εἴρηκα (Perf.)   to say, tell
εἰς   prep.   with acc.: into; against; to, towards
εἷς, μία, ἕν   adj.   one
εἴσειμι   to go into
ἐκ (ἐξ)   prep.   with gen.: from, out of; by
ἐκδέω, -δήσω   to bind, fasten; hang
ἐκκρούω   to drive out
ἐκλάμπω, -ψω   to shine, glow

ἐκπέμπω, -ψω   to send out, send forth, send away

ἐκπετάννυμι, ἐκπετάσω   to spread out, unfurl

ἐκπονέω, ἐκπονήσω, ἐξεπόνησε   to work out, accomplish, labor

ἐκπρολείπω, ἐκπρολείψω, ἐκπρούλιπον   to leave, desert, forsake

ἐκπτύω, -ύσω   to spit out

ἐκτελέω, -έσω   to accomplish, finish

ἐκφαίνω, -φανῶ   to bring to light, reveal

ἐλαία, -ας   f.   the olive tree

ἐλαφρός, -ά, -όν   adj.   light, not burdensome

ἔλεγος, -ου   m.   a lament, song of mourning; mournful, elegaic (as adj.)

ἐλεέω, -ήσω   to have pity on, to pity

ἕλιξ, -ικος   f.   anything twisted, winding or spiral; the tendrils of a vine or of ivy

ἑλίσσω, -ξω   to turn round or about, revolve

ἕλκος, -εος   n.   a wound

ἕλκω, -ξω, εἷλξα   to drag, pull

Ἕλλην, -ηνος   m.   a Greek, Hellene

ἔλλιπον   dialectic 2 Aor. from λείπω

ἐλπίς, -ίδος   f.   hope

ἐμεῦ = ἐμοῦ   gen. sg. from ἐγώ

ἐμός, -ή, -όν   1st person poss. adj.   mine, my

ἔμπαλι   adv.   backwards, back, contrary to

ἐμπλέκω, -ξω   to weave, interweave

ἐμπνέω, -πνεύσω   to blow

ἔμπνοος, -ον   adj.   living, breathing

ἔμπορος, -ον   adj.   a traveller; a merchant

ἔμπυρος, -ον   adj.   scorched, burnt; fiery

ἔμφρων, -ον   adj.   possessed of reason; sensible, wise; alive, vivid

ἔμψυχος, -ον   adj.   living, animated

ἐν   prep.   with dat.: in, among

ἐναγκαλίζομαι -ίσομαι   to take in one's arms

ἐναιχμάζω, -αιχμάσω (-αιχμάσσω)   to fight

ἔναρα, -ων   n. pl.   the arms of a slain enemy, spoils

ἐνειδοφορέω, -ήσω   to mold, shape in stone

ἔνειμι, ἐνέσομαι   to be in or at a place, to be within; to be at home

ἐνελίσσω   to roll or wrap up; to be wrapped in (Pass.)

ἐνέπω   to tell, describe, speak of

ἐνθάδε   adv.   there, here; then, thereupon

ἐννέπω = ἐνέπω

ἐννύχιος, -α, -ον   adj.   nightly, in the night

ἐνοπή, -ῆς   f.   a battle cry

ἐντός   adv.   in, within, inside; between

ἔντρομος, -ον   adj.   trembling, shaking

ἐνύπνιον, -ου   n.   a thing seen in sleep, a dream

ἑός, ἑή, ἑόν   3rd person poss. adj.   his own, her own, its own

ἐπεί   conj.   when, since

ἔπειμι   to go or come towards, approach

ἐπέχω, ἐφέξω, ἐπέσχον   to hold, lay hold upon; to stay, stop, pause (intrans.)

ἐπί   prep.   with gen.: upon
    with dat.: on the terms, on, at; by
    with acc.: against; over, to; with regard to

ἐπιβαίνω, -βήσομαι, ἐπέβην   to set upon; to go upon   (ἐπιβάς 2 Aor. Part.)

ἐπιγράφω, -ψω   to scrape, write upon, inscribe

ἐπιδίδωμι, -δώσω   to give besides; give freely; to assign as one's witness in a thing (Mid.)

ἐπιμαστίδιος, -ον   adj.   at the breast, not weaned

ἐπινυμφίδιος, -ον   adj.   bridal, nuptial

ἐπίορκος, -ον   adj.   swearing falsely, perjured

ἐπιπλέκω, -ξω   to plait or braid in

ἐπιπρέπω   to be conspicuous; to fit, suit

ἐπισκύνιον, -ου   n.   the skin of the brow

ἐπίσταμαι, ἐπιστήσομαι   to be skilled in a thing, to know well

ἐπίτηκτος, -ον   adj.   melted; superficial, false

ἐπιτρέχω, θρέξομαι (1 Fut.), ἐπιδραμοῦμαι (2 Fut.), ἐπέδραμον (2 Aor.)   to run to, at or upon; to overrun, spread over

ἐπιχαιρέκακος, -ον   adj.   rejoicing in one's ills or misfortunes; spiteful

ἕπομαι   dep. Mid. from ἕπω   to follow

ἐπόμνυμι, ἐπομοῦμαι   to swear to, swear upon

ἔπος, -εος   n.   a word, a speech

ἐπουράνιος, -α, -ον   adj.   in heaven

ἕπω, ἕψω   to be about, with

ἐπωνυμία, -ας   f.   a surname

ἐραστός, -ή, -όν = ἐρατός

ἐρατός, -ή, -όν adj. beloved

ἔργον, -ου n. a deed, work; handiwork

ἐρείδω, -είσω to press, force, lean against; to lean oneself against, to be fixed, firm (Mid. and Pass.)

ἐρημολάλος, -ον adj. chattering in the desert or wilderness

ἐρισθενής, -ές adj. mighty, powerful

ἐρκοῦρος, -ον adj. watching an enclosure

ἔρνος, -εος n. a young sprout, shoot

ἔρπυλλον, -ου n. creeping thyme

ἔρπυλλος, -ου m. and f. = ἔρπυλλον

ἔρρω, ἐρρήσω to wander; to go, come

     ἔρρε away with you!

ἔρχομαι, ἐλεύσομαι, ἦλθον, ἐλήλυθα to come, go; to come back, return

ἐρῶ Fut. of εἰπεῖν I shall say

ἔρως, -ωτος m. love

ἐρωτογράφος, -ον adj. writing about love

ἐρωτοπλάνος, -ον adj. beguiling, soothing love

ἐρωτοπλοέω to sail on love's ocean

ἔς = εἰς

ἐσοράω (εἰσοράω), ἐσόψομαι, εἰσεῖδον to look at or upon (ἐσίδῳ 2nd sg. Aor. Mid. Subj.)

     ἐσοράω μή take care (lest)

ἑσπέριος, -α, -ον adj. in the evening

ἕσπερος, -ου m. evening, the evening star

ἐσσί = εἶ 2nd sg. Pres. from εἰμί

ἔσχατος, -η, -ον adj. last; worst; the extreme

ἑταίρα, -ας f. a companion, friend, mistress

ἑταῖρος, -ου m. a companion, friend

ἔταρος, -ου m. = ἑταῖρος

ἕτερος, -α, -ον adj. other, different

ἔτι adv. still, yet

ἔτυμος, -η, -ον adj. true, sure, real

ἐτύμως adv. truly, actually, really

ἔτος, -εος n. a year

εὐάγγελος, -ον adj. bringing good news

εὔαδε 3rd person sg. 2 Aor. from ἀνδάνω it pleases, is agreeable

εὐάνθεμος, -ον adj. flowery, blooming; lovely (like a flower)

εὐδαίμων, -ον adj. fortunate, prosperous, blessed

128

εὕδω, εὑδήσω   to sleep
εὐκαρπέω, ῶ   to abound in fruit, be fruitful, fertile
εὔλαλος, ον   adj.   sweet-spoken
εὐμαθία, ας   f.   readiness to learn, docility
εὐνή, ῆς   f.   a bed, couch
εὐπέταλος, ον   adj.   with beautiful leaves
εὐπλόκαμος, ον   adj.   fair-haired, with beautiful hair
εὑρίσκω, εὑρήσω, εὗρον, εὕρηκα   to find by chance, meet with, dis-
   cover
εὐσεβής, ές   adj.   pious, reverent
εὐστοχέω   to hit the mark; to be successful
εὔστροφος, ον   adj.   curved, curled, twisted
εὔφορτος, ον   adj.   well-freighted
εὐχαίτης, ου   m.   with beautiful leaves or hair
εὔχομαι, εὔξομαι, ηὐξάμην   to pray; to vow, promise; to boast
εὐώδης, ες   adj.   sweet-smelling
     εὐώδης σχοῖνος   ginger-grass
ἐφέζομαι, εδοῦμαι   to sit upon, by or at
ἔφηβος, ον   adj.   arrived at manhood or womanhood
ἐφίπταμαι, επτάμην (Aor.)   to fly upon or towards
ἐφίστημι, ἐπιστήσω, ἐπέστην (2 Aor.)   to set on or over; to place
   upon; to stand over or on (Mid. and intrans. 2 Aor.)
ἐφοράω, ἐπόψομαι   to observe, look out for
ἔχω, ἔξω (σχήσω), ἔσχον, ἔσχηκα   to have, hold
ἐών = ὤν   Pres. Part. from εἰμί

Z

ζάω, ζήσω, ἔζησα   to live, abide
ζῆλος, ου   m.   jealousy
ζηλότυπος, ον   adj.   jealous
Ζήν, Ζηνός   m.   Zeus
ζωή, ῆς   f.   life
ζωογλύφος, ου   m.   a sculptor
ζωός, ή, όν   adj.   alive, living
ζωροποτέω   to drink strong wine

H

ἤ   conj.   or
    ἤ ... ἤ   either ... or
ἦ   adv.   in truth, truly; sometimes used to introduce a question
    ἦ ῥα very truly, really (strengthens the affirmation)
ἥβη, -ης   f.   youth, early manhood
ἠδέ   conj.   and
ἤδη   adv.   already, before this; now, soon
ἥδομαι, ἡσθήσομαι, ἥσθην   to delight, enjoy, satisfy
ἡδυεπής, -ές   adj.   sweet-speaking, sweet-voiced, sweet-sounding
ἡδυμελής, -ές   adj.   sweet-strained, melodious
ἡδύπνοος, -ον   adj.   sweet-breathing, fragrant
ἡδύς, -εῖα, -ύ   adj.   sweet
ἥλιος, -ου   m.   the sun
ἤίθεος, -ου   m.   a bachelor, young man
ἠϊόνες, -ων   f. pl.   the banks, the shore
ἥκω, ἥξω, ἧκα   to be arrived; to concern, relate, belong to
ἧλιξ, -ικος   m.   a comrade (of the same age)
ἤλυθον   dialectic 2 Aor. from ἔρχομαι
ἡμέτερος, -α, -ον   poss. adj.   our
ἥμισυς, ἡμίσεα (-η), ἥμισυ   adj.   half
ἤν (ἐάν)   conj.   with Subj.: if, in case that
ἠνίδε   interj.   see!, see there!
ἡνίκα   adv.   when, at which time
ἡνιοχέω   to hold the reins, guide, govern
ἡνίοχος, -ου   m.   one who governs, sways, guides
ἠοῖος, -α, -ον   adj.   morning
ἠρέμα   adv.   gently, quietly, calmly, softly
ἥσυχος, -ον   adj.   quiet, calm
ἦχος, -ου   m.   a sound, noise
ἠῶος, -ῷα, -ῷον   adj.   at morning, at break of day

Θ

θάλαμος, -ου   m.   an inner room or chamber; the bridal chamber
θάλασσα, -ης   f.   the sea
θαλερός, -ά, -όν   adj.   fresh, young; luxuriant, rich
θάλλω, θαλῶ, ἔθαλον, τέθηλα   to bloom, sprout

θάλος, -εος   n.   a young shoot or branch; an offspring

θάλπω, -ψω   to make warm; to be warm (Pass.)

   θάλπεῦ = θάλπεται

θαμβέω, -ήσω   to be astonished, amazed

θάμβος, -εος   n.   amazement, astonishment

θάνατος, -ου   m.   death

θαρσέω (θαρρέω), -ήσω   to take courage, take heart

θαῦμα, -ατος   n.   a wonder, marvel

θεή, -ῆς   f.   a goddess

θεῖος, θεία, θεῖον   adj.   of divine race or origin, holy

θέλγω, -ξω   to soothe, charm, enchant

θέμις, θέμιστος   f.   custom, that which is right

θεόπαις, -παιδος   m. and f.   child of the gods, divine

θεός, -οῦ   m.   a god, divinity

θερμός, -ή, -όν   adj.   warm, hot

θέρος, -εος   n.   summer; the summer heat

θετός, -ή, -όν   adj.   adopted

θηλυμανής, -ές   adj.   creating passion for women

θῆλυς, θήλεια, θῆλυ   adj.   female, belonging to women

   ἡ θήλεια =   a woman

θήρ, θηρός   m.   a wild beast

θηρίον, -ου   n.   a wild animal, savage beast

θιγγάνω, θίξομαι, ἔθιγον   to touch lightly

θλίβω, θλίψω   to press, press hard, rub

θνατός, -ή, -όν   adj.   mortal, human

θνήσκω, θανοῦμαι, ἔθανον   to die, be dying

θνητός, -ή, -όν = θνατός

θοίνη, -ης   f.   a feast, banquet

θράσος, -εος   n.   boldness, daring

θρασύς, -εῖα, -ύ   adj.   bold, spirited

θρασυστομία, -ας   f.   impudence

θραύω, θραύσω   to break in pieces

θρέμμα, -ατος   n.   a swarm

θρέπτειρα, -ας   f.   a feeder, rearer, nurse

θρεπτήρ, -ῆρος   m.   a feeder, rearer

θριγκός, -οῦ   m.   the topmost course of stones in a wall, the cor-
   nice

θυμός, -οῦ   m.   the soul, life; mind, temper

θύρα, -ας   f.   a door; double or folding doors (in pl.)

Meleager

I

ἰαίνω, ἰανῶ, ἴηνα   to warm, heat; to melt

ἴαμβος, -ου   m.   an iambus (metrical foot); an iambic verse or poem

ἰδέ   conj.   and

ἰδού   adv.   see there!, there!, well!

ἰδοῦ   2nd sg. 2 Aor. Imperat. Mid. from εἴδομαι (ὁράω)

ἰδοῦσα   2 Aor. fem. Part. Act. from εἴδω

ἴδρις, ἴδριος (ἴδρεως)   m. or f.   knowing, skillful, wise

ἱδρύω, -ύσω   to seat; to be seated, sit still (Pass.)

ἱερός, -ά, -όν   adj.   holy, sacred, glorious

ἵημι, ἥσω, ἧκα   to hurl, throw

ἴθι   Imperat. from εἶμι   come!, go!, begone!

ἱκέτης, -ου   m.   a suppliant; fugitive

ἵκω   to come, go, arrive, reach

ἵλαος, -ον   adj.   gracious, gentle

ἱλαρός, -ά, -όν   adj.   cheerful, joyous

ἵλημι   to be gracious, have mercy (ἵλαθι or ἵληθι 2nd sg. Pres. Imperat. Act.)

ἱμείρω   to long for, desire

ἵμερος, -ου   m.   a longing, desire

ἱμερτός, -ή, -όν   adj.   longed for, much desired

ἵνα   conj.   that, in order that

ἰξός, -οῦ   m.   mistletoe; birdlime

ἰοδόκος, -ον   adj.   holding arrows

ἴον, -ου   n.   the violet

   ἴον μέλαν   the black violet

ἰός, -οῦ   m.   an arrow

ἶρις, -ιος (-ιδος, -εως)   f.   the iris

ἴσος, ἴση, ἴσον   adj.   equal to, the same as

ἵστημι, στήσω, ἔστησα (στῆσα), ἔστην (2 Aor.)   to make to stand, set, place; intrans. in 2 Aor.: to stand

ἱστίον, -ου   n.   a sail; cloth

ἱστός, -οῦ   m.   a ship's mast

ἰσχίον, -ου   n.   hip joint; hips or loins (in pl.)

ἰσχύω, -ύσω   to be strong, powerful

ἴχνος, -εος   n.   a footstep, a step

ἰώ   interj.   oh! (an exclamation of fear)

K

Καδμεῖος, -α, -ον   adj.   Cadmean
καθαιρέω, -ήσω, καθεῖλον   to bring down; put down, reduce
καθαρμόζω   to join or fit to
καθεύδω, καθευδήσω   to sleep, to lie
καί   conj.   and, also, even
   καὶ δή   well then
   καὶ μὴν καί   and what is still more
καινός, -ή, -όν   adj.   new, fresh
καίριος, -α, -ον   adj.   seasonable, timely
καίτοι   conj.   and yet, yet
καίω, καύσω   to burn, parch; light, kindle
κἀκ = καὶ ἐκ
κακάγγελος, -ον   adj.   bringing ill tidings
κακίζω, -ίσω   to blame, reproach
κακοπάρθενος, -ου   f.   an evil maiden
κακός, -ή, -όν   adj.   bad, evil, unhappy
καλάμη, -ης   f.   a stalk of corn
καλέω, καλέσω   to call, summon
καλλάϊνος, -η, -ον   adj.   blue-green
κάλλος, -εος   n.   beauty
καλλοσύνη, -ης   f. = κάλλος
καλός, -ή, -όν   adj.   beautiful, lovely, delightful
κάλπις, -ιδος   f.   a cinerary urn
κάλυξ, -υκος   f.   a flower bed
κἀμέ = καὶ ἐμέ
καμπτήρ, -ῆρος   m.   a bend, angle; the turning point in a race
   course
κάμπτω, κάμψω   to bend, curve
κἄπιστος = καὶ ἄπιστος
καρπός, -οῦ   m.   fruit
κάρτα   adv.   very much
   καὶ κάρτα   sure enough, truly
καρύα, -ας   f.   the walnut tree
κατά   prep.   with gen.: down from; upon; concerning
   with acc.: throughout; according to
καταγγέλω, -ελῶ   to announce, declare
καταπλέκω, -ξω   to entwine, weave in

καταφλέγω, -ξω   to burn down, consume

κατέχω, καθέξω (κατασχήσω), κάτεσχον   to hold back, keep back

καὐτή = καὶ αὐτή

καὐτός = καὶ αὐτός

κεῖμαι, κείσομαι   to lie down, be idle or asleep (κείσθω 3rd sg. Imperat.)

κεῖνος, -η, -ον   adj.   that; he, she, it (poet. for ἐκεῖνος)

κείρω, κειρῶ, ἔκερσα, κέκαρμαι, ἐκάρην   to cut

κέλαδος, -ου   m.   a noise; the sound of music

κελαινός, -ή, -όν   adj.   black, dark

κέλης, -ητος   m.   a light sailing vessel

κενεός, -εά, -εόν = κενός

κενός, -ή, -όν   adj.   empty, void; vain, fruitless

κέντρον, -ου   n.   a point, sting, anything piercing

κεράννυμι, κεράσω, ἐκέρασα   to mix, mingle

κέρας, -ατος   n.   a horn (of an animal); a bow

κεραυνοβολέω   to hurl the lightning

κεραυνοβόλος, -ον   adj.   hurling the thunderbolt; thunderbolt (substantive)

κεραυνομάχης, -ου   m.   wielding the thunderbolt

κεύθω, κεύσω, ἔκυθον (2 Aor.), κέκευθα   to bury, conceal, cover up

κἠγώ = καὶ ἐγώ

κἤν = καὶ ἐν

κηρός, -οῦ   m.   wax

κηρύσσω, -ξω   to proclaim, announce

κιθάρα, -ας   f.   a type of lyre or lute

κίκιννος, -ου   m.   curled hair, a ringlet of hair

κινέω, κινήσω   to move, set in motion, stir

κίνησις, -εως   f.   a moving or being moved; emotion, excitement

κισσός, -οῦ   m.   ivy

κλαγγή, -ῆς   f.   the scream of birds; a scream, chirp (any sound respective to each animal that produces it)

κλάδος, -ου   m.   a young shoot, branch

κλάζω, κλάγξω   to make a loud noise

κλαίω, κλαύσομαι   to cry, weep

κλεινός, -ή, -όν   adj.   famous, renowned, illustrious

κλῆμα, -ατος   n.   a branch, shoot or twig (especially of a vine)

κλίνω, κλινῶ, ἔκλινα, κέκλιμαι (Perf. Pass.)   to make bend or bow; to make recline; to lean, rest, lie down, recline (Pass.)

κλισία, -ας   f.   a bed

κλύω   to hear

κλῶν, κλωνός   m.   a young shoot, twig, branch

κλωνίον, -ου   n.   a small shoot, sprout, twig

κλώψ, κλωπός   m.   a thief

κνίζω, κνίσω   to scrape, to scratch; to tease

κνίσμα, -ατος   n.   that which is scraped off; a scratching, itching

κνώδαλον, -ου   n.   a wild, dangerous animal, a beast

κοίλη, -ης   f.   a hollow

κοιμάω, -ήσω   to put to sleep, to lull; to fall asleep (Pass.)

κοιμίζω, -ίσω   to put to sleep, lay to rest

κοινός, -ή, -όν   adj.   common, shared in common

κοίτη, -ης   f.   a bed, couch

κοῖτος, -ου   m.   a going to bed, a sleeping

κόλαξ, -ακος   m.   a flatterer

κόλπος, -ου   m.   the lap, bosom; a fold

κόμη, -ης   f.   foliage, leaves of trees and plants, needles of pine

κομίζω, -ίσω   to take up and carry away; to escort; to take care of

κόνις, -ιος   f.   dust, ashes

κόπτω, κόψω   to strike, cut

κόρη, -ης   f.   a girl, maiden

κόρυμβος, -ου   m.   a cluster

κορυφή, -ῆς   f.   the highest point, top

κορώνη, -ης   f.   a sea-crow

κορωνίς, -ίδος   f.   a garland, wreath; anything curved, rolled or bent; the flourish of the pen

κοσμέω, -ήσω   to arrange, order; adorn

κόσμος, -ου   m.   the world or universe

κού = καὶ οὐ

κοῦρος, -ου   m.   a boy, a son

κοῦφος, -η, -ον   adj.   light, nimble

κραδία, -ας   f.   the heart

κράζω, κεκράξομαι, ἔκραγον   to scream, cry

κράς, -ατός   m.   the head

κράτος, -εος   n.   power; victory

κρέκω   to strike, beat; to play an instrument

κρεμάννυμι, κρεμάσω, ἐκρέμασα   to hang up, suspend

κρέσσων, -ον   adj.   better, surpassing

κρίνον, -ου   n.   the lily

κρόκος, -ου m. the crocus

κρόταλον, -ου n. a rattle

κρόταφος, -ου m. the temple of the head, the brow

κρύπτω, κρύψω to hide, conceal

κτείνω, κτενῶ, ἔκτεινα to kill, slay

κτύπος, -ου m. a loud noise, a crash

κύαμος, -ου m. a bean

κύανος, -ου f. the blue cornflower

κυβεύω to play at dice; to run a risk

κύβος, -ου m. a cube; a die (dice in pl.)

κυκλόω, κυκλώσω to encircle, surround, bend around

κύλιξ, -ικος f. a drinking cup

κυλίω to roll, roll on or in

κῦμα, -ατος n. the swell of the sea; a wave

κύπρος, -ου f. henna

κυρτόω to curve, bend, arch

κύων, κυνός m. and f. a dog, hound

κῶλον, -ου n. a limb (especially the leg or foot)

κωμάζω, -άσω to revel, celebrate

κῶμος, -ου m. a jovial festivity, revel

κώνωψ, -ωπος m. a gnat, mosquito

κωφός, -ή, -όν adj. dull; deaf

Λ

λαβρίς, -ίδος f. a holder, forceps, clasp

λάβρος, -ον adj. furious, hot, fierce

λαγών, -όνος, m. and f. a cleft, hollow

λάθα, -ας f. = λήθη

λάθριος (λαθραῖος), -ον adj. secret, hidden

λαλέω, -ήσω to talk, chatter; utter sounds

λάληθρος, -ον adj. talkative, vocal, prattling

λάλιος, -ία, -ιον = λάλος

λάλος, -ον adj. talkative, babbling

λαμβάνω, λήψομαι, ἔλαβον to take; receive; catch, get hold of

λαμπάς, -άδος f. a torch, lamp

λαμπρός, -ά, -όν adj. brilliant; magnificent, splendid

λάμπω, -ψω (-ψομαι) to give light, shine; to be bright, radiant

λαμυρός, -ά, -όν adj. wanton, hungry

λανθάνω, λήσω, ἔλησα, ἔλαθον (2 Aor.), λέληθα, λέλησμαι, ἐλήσθην
   to escape notice

λάξ adv. with the heel, stamping on

λάσταυρος, -ου m. one who has sexual desire (epithet for a
   κίναιδος)

λέγω, λέξω, ἔλεξα to speak, tell

λείβω, -ψω to pour, let flow; to flow, run (Mid.)

λειμών, -ῶνος m. a meadow, pasture

λείπω, -ψω, ἔλιπον, λέλοιπα, λέλειμμαι, ἐλείφθην to leave, release

λείριον, -ου n. the white lily

λείψανον, -ου n. a piece; remains, remnants (in pl.)

λευκανθής, -ές adj. having white blossoms

λεύκη, -ης f. the white poplar

λευκόϊον, -ου n. the white violet

λευκοπάρειος, -ον adj. fair-cheeked

λευκός, -ή, -όν adj. white

λεύσσω, λεύσω, ἔλευσα to gaze upon, see

λέων, -οντος m. a lion

λήγω, -ξω to allay, appease; to cease, end (intrans.)

λήθαργος, -ον adj. forgetful, lethargic

λήθη, -ης f. forgetfulness

λῆμα, -ατος n. will, desire; spirit; arrogance, pride

ληρέω to speak or act foolishly

λιγυπτέρυγος, -ον adj. chirping with the wings (like a locust)

λίθος, -ου m. a stone

λίμνη, -ης f. a lake

λίνον, -ου n. a flaxen cord; a net

λιπόπνοος (λιπόπνους), -ου (-ουν) adj. breathless, scant of
   breath

λίσσομαι = λίτομαι

λίτομαι, λίσομαι, ἐλισάμην to beg, beseech

λιτός, -ή, -όν adj. prayerful; simple, plain

λίχνος, -η, -ον adj. greedy, eager

λογισμός, -οῦ m. a reckoning, computation, calculation, con-
   sideration

λόγος, -ου m. a word; a saying, account; literature; reason

λοίδορον, -ου n. abuse

λοιπόν adv. for the rest, further

λοιπός, -ή, -όν adj. remaining

λοπάς, -άδος   f.   a dish or plate
λύγξ, λυγκός   m.   a lynx
λύθρον, -ου   n.   defilement of blood; blood
λύκος, -ου   m.   a wolf
λύρα, -ας   f.   a lyre
λυσίπονος, -ον   adj.   releasing from toil
λυχνίς, -ίδος   f.   a plant with a bright red flower, the rose-campion
λύχνος, -ου   m.   a light, lamp
λύω, λύσω, ἔλυσα, λέλυκα, λέλυμαι, ἐλύθην   to loosen, unfasten, release
λωτός, -οῦ   m.   the lotus; a flute

M

μάγειρος, -ου   m.   a cook
μαγεύω   to enchant, apply magic
μαινάς, -άδος   f.   causing madness, intoxicating
μάκαρ, -αρος   m.   blessed, happy, fortunate
μακρός, -ά, -όν   adj.   long; far, distant
μάλα   adv.   very, very much, exceedingly
μᾶλλον   comp. adv.   more, rather
μανθάνω, μαθήσομαι, ἔμαθον   to learn
μαραίνω, -ανῶ, ἐμάρηνα, ἐμαράνθην (Aor. Pass.)   to die away; to decay, fade, wither (Pass.)
μαρτυρία, -ας   f.   a witness; evidence
μάστιξ, -ιγος   f.   a whip
μαστός, -οῦ   m.   the breast (especially of a woman)
μάταιος, -α, -ον   adj.   idle, foolish, useless
μάτην   adv.   in vain
μάτηρ, ματρός   f.   mother
μάχη, -ης   f.   a battle, fight
μέγας, μεγάλη, μέγα   adj.   large, great
μεγαυχής, -ές   adj.   very boastful, proud
μεθαρμόζω, -σω   to change, alter
μεθύσκω, -ύσω   to make drunk, intoxicate
μέθυσος, -η, -ον   adj.   drunk with wine
μειδάω, -ήσω   to smile
μείδημα, -ατος   n.   a smile

μελαμπέταλος, -ον   adj.   dark-leaved

μέλας, μέλαινα, μέλαν   adj.   black, dark

μελετάω, -ησω   to care for, attend

μελέτη, -ης   f.   care, attention

μέλι, -ιτος   n.   honey

μέλισμα, -ατος   n.   a song, melody, tune

μέλισσα, -ης   f.   honey; a bee

μελίστακτος, -ον   adj.   dropping honey

μελίχρους, -ουν   adj.   honey-colored

μέλλω, μελλήσω, ἐμέλλησα   to be on the point of doing some-
thing; to be about to do; to delay, hesitate

μέλος, -εος   n.   a limb; a song, melody

μέλπω   to sing

μέν   part.   indeed (emphasizes preceding word)

   μέν ... δέ   on the one hand ... on the other hand

μένω, μενῶ, ἔμεινα   to stay, remain; await

μέριμνα, -ης   f.   care, thought, trouble

μεσημβρινός, -ή, -όν   adj.   belonging to noon

μεστός, -ή, -όν   adj.   full, sated

μεταξύ   adv.   between; meanwhile; during (with gen.)

μεταρρυθμίζω, -ίσω   to remodel, transform

μετάφρενον, -ου   n.   the back (anatomical)

μέτρον, -ου   n.   a measure; meter; a verse

μή   adv.   not

   conj.: that ... not, lest

μηδέ   adv.   nor, not even, not

   μηδέ ... μηδέ neither ... nor

μηδείς, μηδεμία, μηδέν   adj.   not even one, no one, nothing

μηκέτι   adv.   no more, no longer, no further

μήν   adv.   yes, indeed, truly

μηνύω, -ύσω   to reveal, betray; to make known

μήποτε   adv.   lest ever, that never

μήτηρ, μητρός (μητέρος)   f.   mother

μιαιφονία, -ας   f.   bloodguiltiness, a murderous person

μίγα   adv.   mixed

μίγνυμι, μίξω   to mix, mingle

μικρός, -ά, -όν   adj.   small, little, few

μίμημα, -ατος   n.   anything imitated, a copy

μίμνω = μένω

μίσγω = μίγνυμι

μίτος, -ου m. a thread, string; track

μιτόω to weave

μναμόσυνον, -ου n. = μνημόσυνον

μνῆμα (μνᾶμα), -ατος n. a memorial, remembrance; monument

μνήμη, -ης f. a remembrance, memory

μνημόσυνον, -ου n. a remembrance, memorial, keepsake

μόγις, adv. with difficulty; hardly, scarcely

μοῖρα, -ας f. fate, destiny

μόλις adv. = μόγις

μόνος, -η, -ον adj. alone, only

μορφή, -ῆς f. form, shape; beauty

μοῦνος = μόνος

μοῦσα, -ης f. music, song
    ἡ Μοῦσα the Muse, goddess of the arts

μουσοπόλος, -ον adj. serving the Muses

μόχθος, -ου m. hard work, hardship

μῦθος, -ου m. a word, speech; story

μυῖα, -ας f. a fly

μυροβόστρυχος, -ον adj. with perfumed hair

μύρον, -ου n. sweet-oil, perfumed scent

μυρόπνους, -ουν adj. sweetly scented

μυρόρραντος, -ον adj. wet with unguent, dripping with scent

μυροφεγγής, -ες adj. shining with unguent

μυρραῖος, -ον adj. smelling of myrrh

μύρτος, -ου f. myrtle

μύστης, -ου m. one initiated

μυχθίζω to snort, sneer

N

ναί adv. yes, truly
    ναὶ μά used in affirmative oaths
    ναὶ μήν indeed, truly (strengthens affirmation)

ναίδιος Phoenician equivalent to χαῖρε

ναίω to dwell, inhabit; to lie, be situated (Pass.)

νᾶμα, -ατος n. anything flowing, a stream

ναός, -οῦ m a dwelling, temple

νάρδος, -ου   f.   spikenard

νάρκισσος, -ου   m.   narcissus (the flower)

νᾶσος (νῆσος), -ου   f.   an island

ναύκληρος, -ου   m.   a ship-master; commander, captain

ναῦς, νεώς   f.   a ship (νᾶες or νέες nom. pl.; νηός gen. sg.)

ναύτης, -ου   m.   a sailor, a companion by sea

νέκταρ, -αρος   n.   nectar

νεκτάρεος, -έα, -εον   adj.   of nectar; fragrant

νέκυς, -υος   m.   a dead body, the dead (νεκύεσσι dat. pl.)

νεόγραφος, -ον   adj.   newly painted or written

νεοθαλής, -ές   adj.   fresh-sprouting, youthful

νέος, -α, -ον   adj.   young, new; strange; a young man or woman
    (substantive)

νέρθε(ν)   adv.   underneath, beneath; as prep. with gen.: under

νεῦμα, -ατος   n.   a sign, nod of assent, approval

νήπιος, -α (-η), -ον   adj.   childish; an infant (substantive)

νήσος, -ου = νᾶσος

νήχομαι, νήξομαι   to swim

νίζω, νίψω   to wash

νικάω, -ήσω   to conquer, win

νίκη, -ης   f.   a victory

νίν   acc. sg. of 3rd person pers. pron. = αὐτόν, αὐτήν, αὐτό

νίπτρον, -ου   n.   water (for washing)

νίπτω = νίζω

νοέω, -ήσω, ἐνόησα   to see; perceive, notice

νόος, -ου   m.   mind, disposition, mood

νόσος, -ου   f.   sickness, disease

νοτίζω, -ίσω   to moisten, wet

νότος, -ου   m.   the south wind

νοῦσος, -ου   f. = νόσος

νύ = νῦν

νύμφη, -ης   f.   a nymph

νῦν   adv.   now

νύξ, νυκτός   f.   night

νῶτον, -ου   n.   the back (anatomical); pl. often used as sg.

Ξ

ξανθός, -ή, -όν   adj.   yellow
ξένη (ξείνη), -ης   f.   a foreign land
ξένιος (ξείνιος), -α, -ον   adj.   belonging to a friend or guest
ξένος (ξεῖνος), -ου   m.   a stranger, guest
ξίφος, -εος   n.   a sword
ξυνός, -ή, -όν   adj.   common, mutual

Ο

ὅδε, ἥδε, τόδε   demonstr.   this
ὁδός, -οῦ   f.   a way, road, path
ὀδύνη, -ης   f.   pain, grief
ὀθόνη, -ης   f.   a sail
οἴαξ, -ακος   m.   the rudder
οἶδα (Perf. with Pres. signif.), ᾔδειν (Pp.)   to know, understand;
      to be able, have the power to (with Infinitive)
οἰκέω, -ήσω   to dwell, inhabit
οἶκος, -ου   m.   a house, dwelling
οἴκτρος, -α, -ον   adj.   pitiable, lamentable; crying
οἰμωγή, -ῆς   f.   weeping and wailing
οἰμώζω   to cry, lament
οἰνάνθη, -ης   f.   a vine; the first shoot of the vine
οἴνη, -ης   f.   a vine, branch
οἰνοβαρής, -ές   adj.   heavy with wine
οἰνοβρεχής, -ές   adj.   soaked in wine, drunken
οἰνόμελι, -ιτος   n.   honey mixed with wine
οἰνοποτέω   to drink wine
οἶνος, -ου   m.   wine
οἰνοχοέω, -ήσω   to pour out wine for drinking
οἰνοχόος, -ον   adj.   pouring out wine to drink; a cupbearer (sub-
      stantive)
οἷος, -α (-η), -ον   rel. pron.   such as, what sort, nature, kind
ὀϊστοβόλος, -ον   adj.   shooting an arrow
ὀϊστός, -οῦ   m.   an arrow
οἰστροβολέω   to strike with a sting (of love)
ὀκτωκαιδεκέτης, -ου   m.   eighteen years old
ὄλβιος, -ον   adj.   happy

ὀλβιστός, -ή, -όν adj.   to be deemed happy, blessed

ὀλίγος, -η, -ον adj.   few, little

ὄλλυμι, ὀλέσω, ὤλεσα   to destroy; to perish, die (Mid.)

ὀλολυγμός, -οῦ m.   a loud crying, wailing

ὅλος, -η, -ον adj.   whole, entire

ὅλως adv.   on the whole; all, completely

ὁμιλέω, -ήσω   to be together, to join; to be in company with

ὄμμα, -ατος n.   the eye

ὄμνυμι, ὀμοῦμαι, ὤμοσα   to swear an oath

ὀμνύω, ὤμνυε (Imperf.) = ὄμνυμι

ὁμόδουλος, -ον adj.   a fellow-slave (substantive); in love with one
    woman (metaph.)

ὁμός, -ή, -όν adj.   common, same

ὁμοῦ adv.   together

ὁμώνυμος, -ον adj.   having the same name; name-sake

ὄνειρον, -ου n.   a dream

ὄνομα, -ατος n.   name, reputation; pretext; word, expression

ὄντως adv.   really, actually

ὄνυξ, -υχος m.   the fingernail

ὀξυβόας, -ου m.   shrill-screaming; shrill- voiced

ὀξύς, -εῖα, -ύ adj.   sharp, keen; shrill

ὀξυτόρος, -ον adj.   piercing, sharp, pointed

ὀπισθοβάτης, -ου m.   a mounting from behind (sexual)

ὁπλίζω, -ίσω, ὤπλισα   to make or get ready

ὅπλον, -ου n.   a tool; a rope; implements of war, arms, weapons
    (in pl.)

ὅπου adv.   where; when; because, since

ὀπτάω, -ήσω   to roast, broil, fry

ὀπτός, -ή, -όν adj.   broiled, burned

ὁράω, ὄψομαι, ἑώρακα, ὦμμαι, ὤφθην   to see; to be seen; appear;
    prove to be (Pass.); (ἰδέσθαι 2 Aor. Inf. Mid.)

ὀργάνιον, -ου n.   a small musical instrument

ὀργή, -ῆς f.   nature, disposition; anger, passion

ὄργια, -ίων n. pl.   secret rites, mysteries

ὀρθρινός, -ή, -όν   in the morning, early, fresh

ὀρθροβόας, -ου m.   the early caller

ὄρθρος, -ου m.   dawn, day-break; the morning star

ὁρίζω, -ίσω   to appoint, to determine, ordain

ὅρκιον, -ου n.   an oath, pledge, surety

143

ὅρκος, -ου   m.   an oath, the witness of an oath
ὅρμος, -ου   m.   an anchorage, harbor
ὄρνις, ὄρνιθος   m. and f.   a bird
ὄρος, -εος   n.   a mountain, hill
ὅρπηξ, -ηκος   m.   a sapling, young shoot or tree
ὅς, ἥ, ὅ   rel. pron.   who, which
ὅσιος, -α, -ον   adj.   hallowed, sanctioned; lawful
ὅσος, -η, -ον   adj.   as great as, as much as
ὅσσος, -η, -ον = ὅσος
ὀσφύς, ὀσφύος   f.   the loin
ὅτε   adv.   when; since
ὅτι   conj.   that
ὅττι = ὅτι
οὐ   neg. adv.   not
οὖας, -ατος   n.   the ear
οὐατόεις, -εσσα, -εν   adj.   long-eared
οὐδέ   adv.   and not, nor yet, not even
οὐκέτι   adv.   no more, no longer
οὖλος, -η, -ον   adj.   whole, entire; thick; twisted
οὖν   adv.   so, then, therefore, accordingly
οὕνεκα   adv.   on which account; since, because
οὔποτε   adv.   never, not ever
οὐρανομήκης, -ες   adj.   reaching to heaven
οὐρεσίφοιτος, -ον   adj.   haunting the mountains or hillsides
οὔριος, -α, -ον   adj.   with a fair wind
οὖρος, -εος   n.   a mountain, hill
οὔτε   conj.   and not, neither, nor
      οὔτε ... οὔτε·   neither ... nor
οὔτις, οὔτι   adj.   no one, nobody, nothing
οὗτος, αὕτη, τοῦτο   demonstr. adj.   this
ὀφείλω, ὀφειλήσω, ὤφελον   to owe; to be due, to be bound (Pass.);
      due, fitting (Pass. Part.)
ὀφθαλμός, -οῦ   m.   the eye; sight; presence
ὄφρα   conj.   that, in order that
ὀφρύς, -ύος   f.   the eyebrow
ὀχέω, -ήσω   to bear, endure; to be carried, borne (Pass.)

Π

πάγη, -ης f. a trap, snare

πάγκαρπος, -ον adj. rich in every fruit, varied in fruit

πάγκοινος, -ον adj. common to all

παίγνιον, -ου n. a plaything; a poem or tune

παιδάριον, -ου n. a little boy

παιδομανής, -ές adj. mad after boys

παιδοφιλέω to love boys

παιδοφόρος, -ον adj. bearing away a boy

παίζω, παίξομαι, ἔπαισα to play

παῖς, παιδός m. and f. a child; son or daughter

πάλαι adv. long ago; formerly

πάλι (ν) adv. back, again

παλίμπους, -οδος m. and f. a returning

παλινδρομία, -ας f. a running back; a returning

πάλλω, ἔπηλα (Aor.) to swing, toss; to leap, bound (Intrans.); to move oneself (Mid.)

παμμήτειρα, -ας f. = παμμήτωρ

παμμήτωρ, -ορος f. mother of all

πάμφυλος, -ον adj. of mingled tribes; of all sorts

πανάγρυπνος, -ον adj. sleepless

παναίσχιστος, -ον superl. adj. ugliest, most shameful or disgraceful

πανδαμάτωρ, -ορος m. all-tamer, able to overcome all things

παννυχίς, -ίδος f. a night festival

πανόδυρτος, -ον adj. most lamentable

πάντοθι adv. everywhere

πάντροφος, -ον adj. all-nourishing

παρά prep. with gen.: from
    with dat.: with, in the presence of, among
    with acc.: to, beyond, contrary to

παραδείκνυμι, -δείξω to hold up to view, represent; to point out

παραδίδωμι, -δώσω, παρέδωκα to give or hand over; to commit

παράκοιτος, -ον adj. sleeping beside

πάραλον, -ου n. a plant that grows by the sea (spurge)

παραμύθιον, -ου n. an exhortation, encouragement; consolation

παραπέτομαι, -πτήσομαι to fly by, fly near

πάρειμι, παρέσομαι, παρῆν (Imperf.) to be present; (impers.) it remains for, it is possible

παρθενικός, -ή, -όν adj. = παρθένιος

παρθένιος, -α, -ον adj. of a maiden or virgin

παρθενόχρως, -ωτος m. and f. maiden-hued, delicate in color

παρίημι, παρήσω, παρείθην (1 Aor. Pass.) to let drop beside, fall beside, place beside; to be relaxed, yield, allow (Mid. and Pass.); παρεθ᾽ = πάρετε (2nd pl. 2 Aor. Imperat. Act.)

πάροιθε (ν) prep. with gen.: before, in the presence of; as adv.: before, in front; formerly

παροικέω, -ήσω to dwell beside, near

πάροικος, -ον adj. dwelling beside or near

πάρος adv. before, in front

πᾶς, πᾶσα, πᾶν adj. all, every; the whole, entire

παστός, -ου m. a bridal chamber; the bridal bed

πάσχω, πείσομαι, ἔπαθον, πέπονθα to experience; suffer

πάταγος, -ου m. a sharp, loud noise, clatter

πατέω, -ήσω to tread upon, tread, walk

πατήρ, πατέρος (πατρός) m. a father

πάτρα (πάτρη), -ας (-ης) f. fatherland, one's country

παύω, παύσω to cease, stop

παχύνω to fatten; to grow fat, be swollen (Pass.)

πέδη, -ης f. a fetter

πέδιλον, -ου n. sandal, shoe (mostly in pl.)

πεζοπόρος, -ον adj. going on foot

πεῖρας, -ατος n. the end, issue

πελαγῖτις, -ιδος f. of or on the sea

πέλαγος, -εος n. the sea

πέλομαι to be (implies a continuance)

πενθέω, -ήσω to lament, mourn

πένθος, -εος n. grief, sorrow

πενιχρός, -ά, -όν adj. poor, needy

πεπαίνω, -ανῶ, ἐπεπάνθην (Aor. Pass.) to ripen; to become ripe or soft (Pass.)

πέρ enclit. part. much, very; however

περάω, περάσω, ἐπέρασα to pass, pass through, cross

περί prep. with gen.: around, about, near; concerning
with dat.: around, for; on account of
with acc.: around, about; in relation to

περιαγής, -ές   adj.   broken in pieces

περίβλεπτος, -ον   adj.   admired, notable

περινήχομαι   to swim around, float about

περισκυθίζω, -ίσω   to scalp; to perform fellatio

περιστείχω, -ξω   to go round about

πέταλον, -ου   n.   a leaf

πέτασος, -ου   m.   a broad-brimmed hat

πέτομαι, πετήσομαι (πτήσομαι), ἐπτόμην (ἐπτάμην)   to fly
   (πταίης   2nd sg. 2 Aor. Opt. Act.; πέτου 2nd sg. Pres.
   Imperat.)

πέτρος, -ου   m.   a stone

πεύθομαι, πεύσομαι = πυνθάνομαι

πεύκη, -ης   f.   the fir tree; a torch

πῇ   interrog. part.   how?

πῆγμα, -ατος   n.   anything fastened or joined together

πήγνυμι, πήξω, ἔπηξα, πέπηγα   to make fast, fix; make solid

πηδάλιον, -ου   n.   a rudder

πηκτίς, -ίδος   f.   a lyre; a 20-stringed harp

πήληξ, -ηκος   f.   a helmet

πίεσμα, -ατος   n.   anything pressed or squeezed

πικρός, -ά, -όν   adj.   sharp, piercing, bitter

πινυτός, -ή, -όν   adj.   wise, prudent

πίνω, πίομαι, ἔπιον, πέπωκα   to drink (πιεῖν Aor. Inf.)

πιπράσκω, πεπράσομαι (Fut. Perf. Mid.)   to sell

πίπτω, πεσοῦμαι, ἔπεσον   to fall

πιστός, -ή, -όν   adj.   faithful, trusty, loyal

πίτυς, -υος   f.   a pine tree

πλάζω, πλάγξω, ἔπλαγξα   to make to wander, lead astray; to go
   astray, wander (Pass.)

πλαστός, -ή, -όν   adj.   fabricated, counterfeit

πλαταγέω, -ήσω   to clap, clap the hands, to clash

πλατάνιστος, -ου   f.   a plane-tree

πλάτανος, -ου   f.   a plane-tree

πλάττω, πλάσω, ἔπλασα   to form, shape, fashion

πλέον = πλεῖον

πλείων, πλεῖον   adj.   more

   τί δὲ τὸ πλέον   what is the advantage?

   τί δὲ πλέον   what help is it?

πλέκω, πλέξω   to weave, twist, enfold

πλευροτυπής, -ές   adj.   beating the sides, striking the ribs

πλέω, πλεύσω   to sail

πλέων, πλέον = πλείων

πλημμύρω (πλημμυρέω)   to overflow, pour over

πλήρης, -ες   adj.   full of, filled with

πλόκαμον, -ου   n.   a lock of hair

πλόκαμος, -ου   m.   a lock or curl of hair

πλώτης, -ου   m.   a seaman

πλωτός, -ή, -όν   adj.   sailing

πνεῦμα, -ατος   n.   breath, spirit, soul

πνέω, πνεύσω, ἔπνευσα   to blow, breathe

ποδαπός, -ή, -όν   adj.   from what country, from where

ποδηγός, -όν   adj.   guiding the foot; a guide (substantive)

ποθεινός, -ή, -όν   adj.   longed-for, desired

ποθέω, ποθήσω   to long for, desire; to regret

πόθος, -ου   m.   a longing, desire

ποῖ   interrog. adv.   where?

ποικίλος, -η, -ον   adj.   varied, changing, versatile

ποιμήν, -ένος   m.   a shepherd

πόλεμος, -ου   m.   a war, battle

πολιός, -ά, -όν   adj.   grey, white (especially the hair)

πόλις, -εως   f.   a city; country

πολλάκι(ς)   adv.   many times, often

πολύκλαυτος, -η, -ον   adj.   much lamented

πολύπαις, -παιδος   m. and f.   with many children

πολύς, πολλή, πολύ   adj.   many, much

   οἱ πολλοί   the masses

πόνος, -ου   m.   hard work, toil; pain, suffering

πόντος, -ου   m.   the sea

πορεύω, -εύσω   to bring, carry; to go, travel (Mid.)

πορθμεύω   to carry over, carry away (πορθμευθείς Aor. Pass. Part.)

πόρος, -ου   m.   a strait, means of passing

   πόρος Ἕλλης   the Hellespont

πορφύρεος, -α (-η), -ον   adj.   purple

ποτέ   enclit. part.   sometime, anytime, once, ever

ποτί = πρός

πότνια   f.   lady, mistress (a title of honor for a female)

που   enclit.   anywhere, somewhere; perhaps

ποῦ   interrog. adv.   where? how? in what manner?

πουλυετής, -ές adj. lasting many years, full of years (πολύς + ἔτος)

πούς, ποδός m. foot (ποσσί dat. pl.)

πρᾶτος, -α, -ον = πρῶτος

πρέσβυς, -υος (-εως) m. an old man

πρεσβύτης, -ου m. an old man

πρίν adv. before, formerly

πριονώδης, -ες adj. saw-like

πρό prep. with gen.: before

προάγω, -άξω to lead before, lead on; to escort

πρόγονος, -ον adj. earlier born; ancestors (substantive in pl.)

προδότης, -ου m. a traitor

πρόθυρον, -ου n. a front door

προλέγω to pick out, choose; foretell; caution, warn

προπετής, -ές adj. falling forward; on the point of death

προπίνω, προπίομαι, προύπιον to drink before another

προπίπτω, -πεσοῦμαι, προύπεσον to fall forward or upon something

πρός prep. with gen.: from which; towards, against
with dat.: near, at, on
with acc.: towards, to, upon; according to; in comparison

πρόσειμι to go to, approach; to come forward (προσίτω 3rd sg. Pres. Imperat. Act.)

πρόσθε (ν) adv. before, formerly, of old, earlier

προσίπταμαι (προσπέτομαι), προσπτήσομαι to fly towards

προστίθημι, -θήσω to place before; to put forth (πρόσθες 2nd sg. 2 Aor. Imperat. Act.)

προσψιθυρίζω to whisper

προτίθημι, -θήσω to place or set before; to set forth publicly, expose (προύθηκεν 3rd sg. 1 Aor.)

πρότονος, -ου m. a forestay (a rope from the masthead to the bow of a ship)

προφαίνω to bring forth to light; to hold a torch before one

πρόφασις, -εως f. an excuse, pretext

προφεύγω, -ξομαι, προύφυγον to flee from, avoid, escape

προφήτης, -ου m. a prophet

πρυμνήσιος, -α, -ον adj. of a ship's stern
τὰ πρυμνήσια stern cables, ropes

πρώϊμος, -ον adj. early

Meleager

πρῶτα   adv.   first
πρωτόπλους, ᵒουν   adj.   just arrived from a journey
πρωτόγονος, ᵒη, ᵒον   adj.   first born
πρῶτος, ᵒη, ᵒον   adj.   first, earliest
πτανός, ᵃά, ᵒόν   adj.   winged, feathered
πτερόεις, ᵉεσσα, ᵉεν   adj.   feathered, winged
πτερόν, ᵒου   n.   a feather, wing
πτέρυξ, ᵘυγος   f.   a wing; the flight of a bird
πτηνός, ᵗή, ᵒόν   adj.   feathered, winged
πτῆξις, ᵉεως   f.   a crouching, cowering, terror
πτύω, πτύσω   to spit out; to loathe
πτώσσω, ᵡξω   to cower from fear, be frightened, crouch
πυκνά   adv.   much, often
πυκνός, ᵗή, ᵒόν   adj.   close, compact, thick; often, frequent
πύματος, ᵗη, ᵒον   adj.   the hindmost, last; as adv.: at the last, for
    the last time
πυνθάνομαι, πεύσομαι   to ask, inquire; learn; hear, understand
πῦρ, πυρός   n.   fire
πυραυγής, ᵉές   adj.   bright like fire
πυρίβλητος, ᵒον   adj.   struck with fire
πυρίπνοος, ᵒον   adj.   fire-breathing, fiery
πυρσός, ᵒου   m.   a torch
πύρωσις, ᵉεως   f.   a burning, lighting
πωλέω, ᵗήσω   to exchange, barter, sell
πῶς   interrog. adv.   how?, in what way or manner?

P

ῥά   enclitic = ἄρα
ῥαδινός, ᵗή, ᵒόν   adj.   slender, delicate
ῥαίνω, ῥανῶ, ἔρρανα   to sprinkle, spray
ῥέπω, ᵠψω   to incline downwards, fall, incline towards a thing
ῥιπτάζω, ᵃάσω   to throw about; to toss oneself about (Pass.)
    (ῥιπτασθείς Aor. Pass. Part.)
ῥίπτω, ῥίψω, ἔρριχα, ῥερῖφθαι (Perf. Pass.), ἐρρίφθην (Aor. Pass.)
    to throw, cast, hurl
ῥόδον, ᵒου   n.   a rose
ῥοιή (ῥοιά), ᵗῆς (ᵃᾶς)   f.   pomegranate
ῥόπαλον, ᵒου   n.   a club, stick

150

ῥύομαι, ῥύσομαι, ἐρρυσάμην   to rescue, save, deliver

ῥυτίς, ίδος   f.   a wrinkle

Ῥωμαϊκός, ή, όν   adj.   Roman

ῥώμη, ης   f.   strength, force

Σ

σαββατικός, ή, όν   adj.   of the Sabbath

σάββατον, ου   n.   the Sabbath; rest

σαίρω, σαρῶ   to draw back the lips, sneer in mockery, smirk
   (σεσηρώς Perf. Part.)

σάκος, εος   n. a shield

σαλάμ =   salaam

σαλευτός, ή, όν   adj.   shaken, tossed

σάλος, ου   m.   an unsteady, tossing motion; a swell

σάμψυχον, ου   n.   marjoram

σάνδαλον, ου   n.   a sandal

σαρδάνιος, α, ον   adj.   with γελᾶν, laugh bitterly or painfully

σαρκοταχής, ές   adj.   with flesh wasting away

σαρκοφαγέω   to eat flesh

σβέννυμι, σβέσω, ἔσβεσα (σβέσα)   to quench, put out

σελήνη, ης   f.   the moon

σέλινον, ου   n.   celery

σελίς, ίδος   f.   the page of a book

σεῦ = σοῦ

σηκός, οῦ   m.   a sacred enclosure, precinct

σημαίνω, ανῶ   to show by a sign, point out

σθένος, εος   n.   strength

σιβύνης, ου   m.   a hunting spear

σῖγα   adv.   silently

σιγάω, ήσω   to be or keep silent

σίδαρος, ου   m.   iron

σιμός, ή, όν   adj.   snub-nosed

σίσυμβρον, ου   n.   serpolet, water cress

σίφων. ωνος   n.   a syphon
   αἵματος σίφωνες   blood-suckers

σκαπτοῦχος, ον   adj.   bearing of the sceptre, supreme command

σκαπτροφόρος, ον   adj.   bearing a staff or sceptre

σκῆπτρον (σκᾶπτρον), -ου   n.   a staff, sceptre; the badge of command; sovereignty

σκηπτροφορέω   to bear a sceptre

σκηπτροφόρος, -ον = σκαπτροφόρος

σκιερός, -ά, -όν   adj.   shady, shaded

σκολιός, -ά, -όν   adj.   crooked, twisting

σκολιότριχος, -ου   m. and f.   with curled hair or leaves

σκορπίος, -ου   m.   a scorpion

Σκυθικός, -ή, -όν   adj.   Scythian

σκύλλω, ἔσκυλα (Aor.)   to mangle, rend

σκῦλον, -ου   n.   spoils, bounty (usually in pl.)

σκῦφος, -εος   n.   a cup

σός, -ή, -όν   2nd person poss. adj.   your

σοφία, -ας   f.   wisdom

σοφιστής, -οῦ   m.   a sophist

σοφός, -ή, -όν   adj.   clever, skillful, wise

σπαδόνισμα, -ατος   n.   a tearing

σπαίρω (ἀσπαίρω)   to gasp, struggle

σπένδω, σπείσω, ἔσπεισα   to pour, offer

σπεύδω, σπεύσω   to urge on, to press on; hasten

σπλάγχνον, -ου   n.   the entrails, viscera; the heart (metaph.) (mostly in plural)

σποδιά (σποδιή), -ᾶς (-ῆς)   ashes

σπουδάζω, -άσω   to make haste

σπουδή, -ῆς   f.   seriousness, gravity; haste, speed

σταγών, -όνος   f.   a drop

στάλα, -ας   f.   a monument, upright stone, gravestone

σταχυόθριξ, -τριχος   m. and f.   the leaves of which form ears

στάχυς, -υος   m.   an ear of corn

στεῖρος, -α, -ον   adj.   barren, sterile

στείχω, στείξω, ἔστειξα, ἔστιχον (2 Aor.)   to go up, ascend; to go to

στέλλω, στελῶ, ἔστειλα   to get ready; to send; to set out, depart

στενάχω   to groan, sigh

στέργω, στέρξω, ἐστέρχθην (Aor. Pass.)   to love, be content with, approve

στέρνον, -ου   n.   the chest, breast

στέφανος, -ου   m.   a crown, garland

στεφάνωμα, -ατος   n.   a crown, wreath

στέφω, -ψω, ἔστεψα, ἐστέφθην (Aor. Pass.)   to encompass, crown
στολίζω, -ίσω   to make ready, to dress
στόμα, -ατος   n.   the mouth
στοργή, -ῆς   f.   affection, love
στράγξ, στραγγός   f.   a drop
στρεπτός, -ή, -όν   adj.   easily bent or twisted, pliant
στρέφω, -ψω, ἔστρεψα   to twist, turn; change, alter
στυγερός, -ά, -όν   adj.   hated, abhorred
στυφελός, -ή, -όν   adj.   sour, harsh, bitter
σύ; ὑμεῖς (Nom. Pl.)   pers. pron.   you
συγκεράννυμι, -κεράσω   to mix together
σύγκοιτος, -ον   adj.   sharing a bed; a companion in bed (substan-
    tive)
σύγκωμος, -ον   adj.   a companion reveler
συζεύγνυμι, -ζεύξω   to yoke together
σύμβολον, -ου   n.   a sign, token
συμπαίκτης, -ου   m.   a playmate
συμπαίστωρ, -ορος   m.   a playmate
συμπείθω, -πείσω   to persuade along with, help in persuading
σύμπλανος, -ον   adj.   wandering about together; a companion in
    wandering (substantive)
σύμπλεκτος, -ον   adj.   entangled, twined together
συμπλέκω, -ξω   to plait together, weave
σύμφωνος, -ον   adj.   harmonious, in accordance with
σύν   prep.   with dat.: with
συνάπτω, -άψω   to join together
συναρπάζω, -άσω   to snatch and carry away; to be seized and car-
    ried off (Pass.)
συνείρω   to string together
σύνθημα, -ατος   n.   a sign, token
σύνθρονος, -ον   adj.   enthroned with
συνίστωρ, -ορος   m. and f.   knowing along with another, con-
    scious; a confidant
συννεφής, -ές   adj.   cloudy, gloomy
σύντροφος, -ον   adj.   brought up together with; living with
συντροχάζω   to run together, mingle with
συοκτασία, -ας   f.   slaughter of boars, boar-slaying
σῦριγξ, -ιγγος   f.   a musical pipe
Σύριος, -α, -ον   adj.   Syrian

Meleager

Σύρος, -ου   m.   a Syrian
συστολίζω, -ίσω   to put together, link, unite
σφαιριστής, -ου   m.   a ball-player
σφέτερος, -α, -ον   adj.   their, their own
σφίγγω, σφίγξω   to bind tight, bind together
σφιγκτός, -ή, -όν   adj.   tightly bound
σχέτλιος, -α -ον   adj.   cruel, savage
σχίζω, -ίσω   to split, separate
σχοῖνος, -ου   m.   a rush
σωφροσύνη, -ης   f.   good sense, self-control, temperance

T

τἀμά = τὰ ἐμά
τἄμπαλιν = τὸ ἀνάπαλιν or τὸ ἔμπαλιν
τάν = τήν
ταρβέω, -ήσω   to be frightened, fear
ταρσός, -οῦ   m.   any broad, flat surface; the flat part of the wing
    when stretched out
τάφος, -ου   m.   a burial, a grave
τάχα   adv.   quickly, soon
ταχινός, -ή, -όν = ταχύς
τάχος, -εος   n.   speed, swiftness; as adv.: quickly, at once
ταχύπους, -ποδος   m. and f.   swift-footed (ταχύπουν Ac. Sg.)
ταχύς, -εῖα, -ύ   adj.   quick, swift
τε   conj.   and
    τε...τε   both...and
τείνω, τενῶ, ἔτεινα   to stretch, bend; extend, reach (τέτανται 3rd
    Pl. Perf. Mid.)
τεκνόω, -ώσω   to furnish with children; to have children, give
    birth (Pass.)
τέλος, -εος   n.   an end, completion; a religious ceremony, rites
τεός, -ή, -όν = σός
τέρας, -ατος   n.   a wonder, marvel; a monster
τέρμα, -ατος   n.   an end, boundary
τέρμινθος, -ου   f.   terebinth (a flax-like plant which grows on the
    olive tree)
τερπνός, -ή, -όν   adj.   delightful, pleasant, enjoyable
τέρπω, -ψω   to fill, satisfy; delight; to enjoy (Pass.)

τέρψις, -εως   f.   enjoyment, delight

τέττιξ, -ιγγος   m.   a cicada

τετράκι (-ς)   adv.   four-times

τεύχω, τεύξω, ἔτευξα, τέτυκον (2 Aor.), τέτευχα, τέτυγμαι, ἐτύχθην   to make, construct, create; that which has been made; i.e. existing, is (Perf. Pass. Part.)

τέφρα (τέφρη), -ας (-ης)   f.   ash, ashes

τήκω, τήξω, ἔτηξα, ἐτάκην (2 Aor.)   to melt, melt down

τηλόθι   adv.   far, afar, at a distance

τιθασός, -όν   adj.   tame, tamed

τίθημι, θήσω, ἔθηκα, τέθηκα, τέθειμαι, ἐτέθην   to place, put, set (θήκατο 3rd Sg. 1 Aor. Mid.; θέτο 3rd Sg. 2 Aor. Mid.; θέσθαι 2 Aor. Inf. Mid.)

τίκτω, τέξω, ἔτεκον, τέτοκα   to bring into the world, bear, give birth, bring forth (τεκεῖν 2 Aor. Inf.; τεκῶν 2 Aor. Part.)
   ἡ τεκοῦσα   the mother

τις, τι   enclitic indef. pron.   some, any; someone, anyone

τίς, τί   interrog. pron.   who?, what?; why?

τιτθός, -οῦ   m.   the nipple of the breast

τιτρώσκω, τρώσω, ἔτρωσα   to wound, hurt

τλάω, ἔτλην (Aor.)   to suffer; to dare

τοιγάρ   infer. part.   so then, therefore, accordingly

τοκεύς, -έως   m.   a father; parents (pl.)

τόλμα (τόλμη), -ας (-ης)   f.   courage, daring

τοξεύω, -σω, ἐτόξευσα, τέτοξα   to shoot with the bow

τόξον, -ου   n.   a bow; bow and arrows (pl.)

τοξότης, -ου   m.   an archer

τορός, -ά, -όν   adj.   clear, distinct, piercing

τόσος (τόσσος), -η, -ον   adj.   so great, so much, so very

τοὐμόν = τὸ ἐμόν

τοὔνεκα (τοὔνεκεν)   adv.   since, for that, because

τοὔνομα = τὸ ὄνομα

τραγόπους, -ποδος   m. and f.   goat-footed

τραῦμα, -ατος   n.   wound, injury

τραχύς, -εῖα, -ύ   adj.   rough, rocky; harsh

τρεῖς (τρισσαί), τρία   adj.   three

τρέπω, τρέψω, ἔτρεψα, ἔτραπον (2 Aor.)   to turn, guide towards a thing; to change, be changed (Pass. and Mid.)

τρέφω, θρέψω, ἔθρεψα   to nourish, rear, nurse

155

τρέχω, δραμοῦμαι, ἔθρεξα, ἔδραμον (2 Aor.)   to run, hurry

τρηχύς, -εῖα, -ύ   adj. = τραχύς

τρίγερων, -οντος   m. and f.   triply old, very old

τριπάνουργος, -ον   adj.   triply evil, an arch-rogue

τρισάλαστος, -ον   adj.   three times cursed

τρισσάκις   adv.   three times

τρισσός, -ή, -όν   adj.   threefold

τρίτος, -η, -ον   adj.   the third

τρόπος, -ου   m.   a turn, direction; a way, manner; character

τροφεῖα   n. pl.   pay for rearing and bringing up, the wages of a
   nurse

τρυγάω, -ήσω   to gather in ripe fruits or flowers

τρυφερός, -ά, -όν   adj.   soft, delicate

τυγχάνω, τεύξομαι, ἔτυχον   to hit; to happen or chance upon; to
   gain, obtain, win (Mid.)

τύμβος, -ου   m.   a grave, tomb; burial

τύπος, -ου   m.   a blow; an impression, stamp, mark, image

τυπόω   to make an impression; mould, model

τυφλός, -ή, -όν   adj.   blind

τύφω, θύψω, ἔθυψα   to smoke, smoulder

τὠτρεκές = τὸ ἀτρεκές

Υ

ὑάκινθος, -ου   m. and f.   hyacinth

ὕβρις, -εως (-ιος)   f.   riotousness, insolence; an outrage, insult

ὑβριστήρ, -ῆρος   m.   a violent, overbearing, or insolent person

ὑγρός, -ά, -όν   adj.   wet, moist

ὕδωρ, ὕδατος   n.   water

υἱός, -οῦ   m.   a son

ὑλακτέω, -ήσω   to yell at; abuse, assail

ὑμέναιος, -ου   m.   a bridal song

ὑμέτερος, -α, -ον   poss. adj.   your, yours

ὑμνοθέτης, -ου   m.   composer of hymns, lyric poet; (as Adj.) of
   poetry, of works of poets

ὑμνοπόλος, -ον   adj.   poet, minstrel

ὕμνος, -ου   m.   song

ὑπένερθε   adv.   under, beneath

ὑπέραντλος, -ον   adj.   full of water, overflowing

ὑπναπάτης, -ου m. sleep-cheating

ὕπνος, -ου m. sleep

ὑπνόω, -ώσω to lull to sleep; to sleep (Pass.)

ὑπό prep. with gen., dat., and acc.: from under, under; with passive verbs: by, at the hands of (agency)

ὑποθάλπω, -ψω to heat inwardly; to glow under, smoulder (Pass.)

ὑποκάω to burn up

ὑπολάμπω, -ψω to shine under; begin to shine

ὑπόπτερος, -ον adj. feathered, winged

ὑποστορέννυμι, -στορέσω to spread or lay under, to lay low

ὑπόχρως, -χρωτος n. underskin; flesh-pressing

ὑφαρπάζω, -άσω to snatch away from under; to filch

ὑφηγέομαι, -ήσομαι to guide, lead; to instruct in a thing

ὑφίστημι, ὑποστήσω, ὑπέστην (2 Aor.) to place or set under; to stand under, stand one's ground (Pass., 2 Aor. and Perf. Act.)

Φ

φαέσφορος, -ον adj. light-bringing

φαιδρός, -ά, -όν adj. bright, joyous

φαίνω, φανῶ, ἔφηνα to bring into sight, make to appear

φαμί = φημί

φανίον, -ου n. a little torch

φαντάζω, -άσω to make visible, clear; to present, represent an object to one's self (Mid.)

φαρέτρη, -ης f. a quiver for arrows

φαρετροφόρος, -ον adj. bearing a quiver

φάσμα, -ατος n. an apparition, phantom

φάτις, -εως (-ιος) f. a saying, report; speech, language

φέγγος, -εος n. light, splendor, daylight

φείδομαι, φείσομαι to spare; to draw back from, turn away from

φέρω, οἴσω, ἤνεγκα (ἤνεγκον), ἐνήνοχα, ἐνήνεγμαι, ἠνέχθην to carry, bear, bring, support, violate; to win (Mid.); to be carried on, be carried about, be in circulation, rush (Pass.)

φεύγω, φεύξομαι, ἔφυγον to flee, escape

φημί, ἔφην (Imperf.), φήσω, ἔφησα to declare, speak, say

φθέγγομαι, -ξομαι, ἐφθεγξάμην to speak loud and clear, cry aloud; sing

φθέγμα, -ατος n. a saying, word, sound

157

φθίω (φθίνω) to decay, waste away, perish (φθίμενος Pass. Part.: slain, dead)

φθόγγος, -ου m. voice

φθόγγον μιτώσασθαι to let one's voice sound like a string, to weave a song

φιλάβουλος, -ον adj. willfully unadvised, lover of ignorance

φιλάγρυπνος, -ον adj. wakeful

φιλάκρητος, -ον adj. fond of wine, wine-loving

φιλάσωτος, -ον adj. fond of debauchery or an unwholesome life

φιλέραστος, -ον adj. loving, amorous

φίλερως, -ωτος m. and f. prone to love, full of love

φιλέω, -ήσω, ἐφίλησα to love; to kiss

φίλημα, -ατος n. a kiss

φιλία, -ας f. friendship, affection

φίλιος, -α, -ον adj. friendly; beloved

φιλόκωμος, -ον adj. fond of feasting and dancing

φίλομβρος, -ον adj. rain-loving, fond of rain or moisture

φιλόμουσος, -ον adj. loving the muses, loving the arts

φιλόπαις, -παιδος m. and f. loving boys

φίλος, -η, -ον adj. loving, dear; friend (as substantive); φίλα (neuter pl.): welcome news

φιλοφροσύνη, -ης f. friendliness, affection

φίλτρον, -ου n. a love charm, spell

φλέγω, φλέξω to burn, set fire

φλόξ, φλογός f. a flame; phlox (the flower)

φοῖνιξ, -ικος m. a palm tree

Φοῖνιξ, -ικος m. a Phoenician

φοιτάω, -ήσω to go in and out; to visit

φόνος, -ου m. murder, bloodshed; blood

φορβή, -ῆς f. fodder, food

φορέω, -ήσω to bear, carry; to possess

φράζω, φράσω, ἔφρασα to make a sign with the hand; to speak, tell

φρενοληστής, -οῦ m. a thief of the understanding or sanity, a deceiver

φρήν, φρενός f. the midriff; the heart; the senses, mind, spirit

φροντίς, -ίδος f. thought, care, attention

φρύαγμα, -ατος n. insolence, arrogance

φρυάσσομαι, -ξομαι to be haughty, insolent; to sneer

φύλαξ, -ακος m. and f.   a guard

φυλάσσω, φυλάξω   to watch, keep guard

φύρω, φύρσω, πέφυρμαι (Perf. Mid.)   to mix together, mingle; to soil, defile; to confuse

φύω, φύσω, ἔφυσα, ἔφυν (2 Aor.)   to bring forth, produce, put forth; to grow, spring up (Pass.)

φωλεός, -ου m.   a den, nest

φωνέω, -ήσω   to speak loud or clearly

φώς, φωτός m.   a man, a mortal

φῶς, φωτός n.   light, ray of light

X

χαίρω, χαιρήσω, ἐχάρην   to rejoice, please, delight   χαῖρε (Imperat.):   hail!, welcome

χαίτη, -ης f.   long, flowing hair

χαλά (χηλή), -ᾶς (-ῆς) f.   anything forked, parted or wrinkled

χαλάω, -άσω   to make slack, to loosen

χαλινός, -οῦ m.   the bit of a bridle, the bridle

χαλκόδετος, -ον adj.   brass-bound, brazen

χαράσσω, -ξω   to scratch, inscribe, write

χαρίεις, χαρίεσσα, χαρίεν adj.   pleasing, lovely, charming

χαρίζομαι, χαρίσομαι, ἐχαρισάμην, κεχάρισμαι   to show kindness, gratify, favor someone   κεχαρισμένος (Perf. Part. Pass.): agreeable, charming

χάρις, -ιτος f.   thanks, a favor, reward, kindness (χάριν Ac. Sg.)

χαροπός, -ή, -όν adj.   bright-eyed; light blue-eyed

χεῖλος, -εος n.   the lip

χεῖμα, -ατος n.   winter, cold

χειμαίνω, -ανῶ   to toss around

χειμέριος, -α, -ον adj.   wintry, stormy

χείρ, χειρός f.   hand, arm

χειροτυπής, -ές adj.   striking with the hands
     χειροτυπῆς πάταγος   clapping of hands

χερός = χειρός

χέρσος, -ου m. and f.   dry land

χέω, χεύσω, ἔχεα, κέχυκα, κέχυμαι, ἐχύθην   to pour

χθιζός, -ή, -όν adj.   of yesterday

χθών, χθονός f.   the earth, ground, soil

χίμαρος, -ου   m.   a male goat

χιών, -όνος   f.   snow

χλαῖνα, -ης   f.   a cloak, mantle

χλαμύς, -ύδος   f.   a cloak, mantle

χλανίς, -ίδος   f.   an upper garment of wool, mantle

χλιαίνω   to warm; to bask, grow warm (Pass.)

χλοερός, -ά, -όν   adj.   pale green, light green

χορός, -οῦ   m.   a dance

χραίνω, χρανῶ   to smear; to stain, spot

χρίω, χρίσω   to rub, anoint with oil or scent, to smear

χρόνος, -ου   m.   time

χρυσανθής, -ές   adj.   with flowers of gold

χρύσειος, -η, -ον   adj.   golden

χρώς, χρωτός (χροός)   m.   the skin

χώ   contr. for καὶ ὁ

ψ

ψακάς, -άδος   f.   a morsel, bit, drop

ψαύω, ψαύσω   to touch lightly, graze

ψεύδω, ψεύσω   to cheat, deceive

ψεύστης, -ου   m.   a liar

ψυχαπάτης, -ου   m.   beguiling, deluding

ψυχή, -ῆς   f.   life, spirit, soul; heart

ψυχρός, -ά, -όν   adj.   cool, fresh, cold

ὧδε   adv.   so, thus; here

ὠδίς, -ῖνος   f.   the pain of childbirth; pain, labor

ὠκεανός, -οῦ   m.   ocean

ὠκύπτερος, -ον   adj.   swift-winged, swift-flying; swift wings (as substantive in pl.)

ὠκύς, ὠκεῖα, ὠκύ   adj.   fast, swift

ὦμος, -ου   m.   the shoulder

ὠνέομαι, -ήσομαι, ἐωνησάμην, ἐώνημαι   to buy, purchase

ὥρα, -ας   f.   hour; season; prime of life, youth

ὥριμος, -ον   adj.   ripe, in season

ὡς   adv.   so, thus; as; that; how